Corporate Predators

Corporate Predators

The Hunt for Mega-Profits
and the
Attack on Democracy

Russell Mokhiber &
Robert Weissman

Common Courage Press   Monroe, Maine

Library of Congress Cataloging-in-Publication Data

Mokhiber, Russell, 1954–
    Corporate predators : the hunt for mega-profits and the attack on
democracy / Russell Mokhiber & Robert Weissman.
      p.   cm.
    Includes index.
    ISBN 1-56751-159-7 (cloth). -- ISBN 1-56751-158-9 (pbk.)
    1. Commercial crimes--United States. 2. Corporations--United
States--Corrupt practices. 3. Union busting--United States. 4.
Sweatshops--United States. [1. Business and politics--United States.
2. Corporations--United States--Political activity.]
    I. Weissman, Robert. II. Title.
HV6769.M652 1999
364.16'8'0973--dc21
                        99-17255
                           CIP

Common Courage Press
Box 702
Monroe, ME 04951

www.commoncouragepress.com

207-525-0900   fax: 207-525-3068

Second Printing

Contents

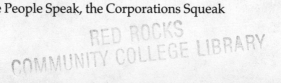

Part IV: Corporation Nation

Part V: The Big Boys Unite
Merger Mania in the 1990s

Part VI: Commercialism Run Amok

Introduction

For the past twenty years, after a decade and a half of populist resurgence against corporate abuses by consumer, environmental, women's rights and civil rights forces, big business has been on a rampage to control our society. Whether these business supremacies are called corporatization, commercialism, monopolies or the corporate state, the overall concentration of power and wealth in ever fewer multinational corporate centers is a matter of record.

In arena after arena—government, workplace, marketplace, media, environment, education, science, technology—the dominant players are large corporations. What countervailing forces that our society used to depend upon for some balance are not in retreat against the aggressive expansion of corporate influence far beyond its traditional mercantile boundaries?

The enlarged power that corporations deploy to further increase their revenues and socialize their costs comes from many sources—new and old. Roughly eighty percent of the money contributed to federal candidates comes from business interests. The mobility to export capital has given transnational companies major leverage against local, state and federal officials, not to mention against organized and unorganized labor. The swell of corporate welfare handouts has reached new depths. The contrived complexity of many financial and other services serves to confuse, deplete and daunt consumers who lose significant portions of their income in a manipulative marketplace. Alliances, joint ventures and other complex collaborations between should-be competitors have made a mockery of what is left of antitrust enforcement.

The opportunities to control or defeat governmental attempts for corporate accountability that flow from transcending national jurisdictions into globalized strategies to escape taxation and pit countries and their workers against one another appear to be endless. The autocratic systems of governance called GATT and NAFTA reflect to the smallest detail ways that giant corporations wish to control the world. These firms are on a collision course against democratic processes, and the merging of states and business, to the latter's advantage, weakens relentlessly both the restraints of the law and the willingness of legislators to do anything about it.

Taken together, the world is witnessing its subjugation to the large corporate model of economic development, the large corporate model of technology and the large corporate model of culture itself. These accelerating trendlines invite accelerating comprehension and response. History demonstrates that commercialism knows few boundaries that are not externally imposed. All the major religions have warned their adherents against the excesses of commercial value systems, albeit with different languages, images and metaphors.

Specific descriptions of corporate misbehavior do nourish proper generalizations that in turn lead to more just movements and practices. Here, columnists Russell Mokhiber and Robert Weissman provide a distinct service in *Corporate Predators*. It is not just the versatility of their writings—covering bribery, pollution, corporate crime, fraud and abuse, failure of law enforcement, union-busting, the mayhem inflicted by product defects and toxics, the deep gap between the rich and the rest of America, corporate front groups, the media censorship and self-censorship, the profiteering, the pillaging overseas and more—but it is also the impact on the reader that comes from aggregating evidence. Our country does not collect statistics on corporate crime the way it does on street crime. For to do so would begin to highlight a little-attended agenda for law enforcement and other corporate reforms. Neither the Congress nor the White House and its Justice Department have made any moves over the years to assemble from around the country the abuses of corporations in quantifiable format so as to drive policy.

So, description—accurate, representational description—must now suffice. As the editor of the *Corporate Crime Reporter*

(Mokhiber) and the editor of the *Multinational Monitor* (Weissman), the authors know well the difference between anecdotes that are illustrative and those that are idiosyncratic. This volume of their weekly columns carries the evidence that illustrates patterns of continuing corporate derelictions, not lonely deviations from a more congenial norm.

The authors' experience over the years with the impact of disclosures has led them to the conclusion that the facts must be linked to civic engagement and democratic activity for change. If disclosure produced its own dynamic imperatives for change, the recurrent exposure of corporate abuses in such mainstream publications as the *Wall Street Journal*, *Business Week* and some national television programs like *Sixty Minutes* would have caused these changes. Such, unfortunately, has not been the case. The linkages between knowledge and action have not been sufficient. But readers of Common Courage Press published books tend toward citizen activism. They want to know because they want to do. Some may even agree with the ancient Chinese saying that "To know and not to do is not to know."

So, go forward readers who wish to be leaders in the advancement of justice—what Daniel Webster once called "the great work of men on Earth"—and savor the writings that will motivate more and more women and men to band together in organizations that build a more just democracy.

Ralph Nader, 1999

Part I
Corporate Crime and Violence

No Mind, No Crime

December 2, 1997

While street crime is reportedly being brought under control in America's major cities, all indications are that corporate crime and violence continue to skyrocket.

Homicide, robbery and burglary are down across the board, but health care fraud, public corruption, environmental crime, securities fraud are enjoying banner years.

The question increasingly being faced now by scholars, citizen activists and policymakers: What to do about runaway corporate crime and violence?

Many federal and state prosecutors believe that corporate crime should be handled like other crime—investigate and prosecute it.

But some scholars, like Jeffrey Parker, a professor of law at George Mason University Law School, argue that corporate crime simply doesn't exist and can't exist.

"Crime exists only in the mind of an individual," Parker said recently. "Since a corporation has no mind, it can commit no crime."

Parker argues that since a corporation is not a person, it should not be treated as people are treated in the criminal law arena.

For this argument, Parker has little support, even among the nation's top white-collar crime defense attorneys.

Why? Corporations realize that if they were to be stripped of their rights to personhood, they would be the big losers. A corporation stripped of its personhood might avoid criminal prosecution, but it would at the same time lose its First Amendment right to speak and associate, its Fourth Amendment right to privacy, and its Fifth Amendment right to protection from double jeopardy.

If corporate crime doesn't exist, what do we call—and how should we handle—all of the pollution, corruption, bribery and fraud that corporations create?

2

Parker argues that "there is no legitimate function of corporate criminal liability that cannot be served equally as well, if not better, by civil enforcement."

At a conference on corporate crime held earlier this year in Washington, D.C., Parker's thesis was challenged head-on by Columbia University Law Professor and corporate criminologist John Coffee.

Coffee agrees that in theory, large civil penalties could work as well as criminal penalties in combatting corporate wrongdoing.

But in practice, they don't work as well because "the civil justice system is very slow and much more favorable to defendants than the criminal justice system."

When it comes to allocating blame, assigning responsibility and shaming wrongdoers, the criminal law works much better than the civil law, Coffee argues.

Coffee argues that if corporations were sanctioned exclusively by civil penalties, their wrongdoing would seem "less blameworthy than the conduct of individuals who were still being processed through the criminal justice system."

"Inevitably, there is a hierarchy between the criminal law, which is seen as front page news, and civil lawsuits, which are on page 17 of the business section," Coffee said.

Coffee's point: since the criminal law is saved for society's most egregious acts, denying the ability to criminally prosecute corporations sends the signal that corporate wrongdoing is not as serious as individual wrongdoing.

Michael Rustad, a professor at Suffolk University Law School in Boston, agrees with Coffee that the criminal law plays an important role in controlling corporate misbehavior, but argues that the wall separating the criminal and civil law is crumbling.

Rustad predicts that the new arena will be that of punitive damages, where corporations will increasingly be hit with heavy penalties for wrongdoing deemed more than mere negligence, but less than what the criminal law requires—intentionally inflicted harm.

Rustad says that corporations rarely, if ever, act maliciously, in the sense that individuals do. Malign neglect is the standard operating procedure in Corporate America. And malign neglect, or reckless disregard, is best dealt with by punitive damages.

With corporate crime and violence inflicting far more damage on society than all street crime combined, it would be a mistake to curb punitive damage awards, as corporate lobbyists are seeking to do in state legislatures around the country, or cut off legitimate criminal prosecutions of corporations, as Parker suggests.

We should take a hard look at the costs of granting corporations the rights of persons and citizens. Should they have the right to define the laws under which they live by lobbying legislatures? Should they have the right to influence elections?

But corporations can't have it both ways. They can't enjoy the benefits of personhood, while at the same time skipping out on its obligations.

Cracking Down on Corruption

November 26, 1997

Pay a bribe, take a tax write-off.

That has long been the rule in Germany and other indus-trialized countries. These nations have not only tolerated bribery of overseas government officials, they have effectively encouraged bribery through tax policies that treat bribes like any other business expense.

Now a new, just-finalized treaty among the rich countries is set to impose a modicum of ethics and sanity on international business practices. The new Anti-Bribery Convention, agreed to by members of the Organization of Economic Cooperation and Development, a grouping of the world's rich nations, requires countries to criminalize bribery of foreign public officials.

The treaty should make a real dent in corruption in devel-oping countries and the countries of the former Eastern Bloc. As Dr. Peter Eigen, chair of Transparency International, an advocacy group that monitors worldwide corruption, notes, a large share of the corruption in developing countries "is the explicit product of multinational corporations, headquartered in leading industrialized countries, using massive bribery and kickbacks to buy contracts in the developing countries and the countries in transition."

Moreover, the treaty among rich nations follows initiatives among developing countries to crack down on corruption. Last year, the Organization of American States—which includes the nations of North and South America—adopted a Convention Against Corruption.

The anti-corruption fight is much more than a do-gooder effort to promote puritanical ethical standards. Corruption exacts a very high toll, especially in the Third World and in the former Eastern Bloc, where resources are tight and the need for governmental services like education and health-care provision are extreme:

- Bribery-induced waste of government resources on boondoggles diverts money from useful government spending on schoolbooks, health clinics and clean water. In Guatemala, for example, the $1.2 billion Chixoy Dam was beset by corruption. It was more than five times over budget, had to be shut for repairs five months after beginning operations in 1983 and has never worked properly since. The World Bank, which supported the project, acknowledges that "with hindsight the Chixoy Dam has proved to be an unwise and uneconomic disaster." Meanwhile, according to the United Nations, more than one-third of Guatemalans go without access to clean water.

- Corruption impedes economic efficiency. A recent Harvard University study found that increasing the corruption level from the rate in Singapore to that of Mexico is equivalent to adding a 20 percent tax on transactions—with none of the proceeds going into public coffers.

- Corruption undermines democracy. In Indonesia, regularly rated one of the most corrupt nations on the planet, President Suharto has extracted bribes and payoffs from foreign investors to enrich his family and cronies. With their newfound wealth, the Suharto clique is now well entrenched as a political, social and economic power elite that will burden Indonesia long after Suharto leaves office.

The anti-corruption campaign is unusual, because it has been underwritten by big corporations in the United States. GE, IBM and Westinghouse are among the leading advocates of an international anti-corruption treaty.

Why have the U.S. companies rallied to the cause? Because the U.S. Foreign Corrupt Practices Act imposes restrictions on American companies' ability to bribe foreign officials. Now the

American companies want to create a level playing field, in which they are not disadvantaged vis-a-vis European and Japanese competitors. This is a rare case that shows how unilateral restrictions on U.S. companies can be effective, not only at curbing U.S. corporate abuses overseas, but at turning American multinational corporations into advocates of enacting those restrictions into international law.

Enforcing and implementing the bribery treaty will be complicated and difficult. Determining the difference between a "bribe" and a "commission" paid to a friend of a high government official can be tricky. But in an era where cynicism rightfully runs rampant over issues of money and politics, the international treaty is a welcome sign that concerted action can work to clean up corruption.

No Shame, No Blame

December 16, 1997

One thing that inside-the-beltway corporate liberals and conservatives agree on is this—crime in America is committed primarily by the poor and the blacks.

Richard Cohen, a *Washington Post* columnist and a corporate liberal, believes that "young black males commit most of the crimes in Washington, D.C."

Charles Krauthammer, a *Washington Post* columnist and a corporate conservative, has written that "crime is generally an occupation of the poor."

James Glassman, a corporate libertarian, writes that the rich "don't commit the violent crimes that require billions to be spent on law enforcement."

These statements can be considered plausible only if we ignore—as Cohen, Krauthammer, Glassman and their colleagues in the mainstream media regularly ignore—the crimes and violence committed by powerful, large American corporations and their primarily wealthy, non-young-black-male executives.

Exactly how much damage is inflicted by corporate crime and violence? Only the criminals, their high-powered lobbyists and lawyers know for sure. (Robert Bennett, one of the nation's premiere white-collar crime defense lawyers, has said that "ninety percent of what I work on never sees the public light of day—and that should be true of any good white-collar crime defense attorney.")

Every year, the Federal Bureau of Investigation (FBI) issues its *Crime in the United States* report which documents murder, robbery, assault, burglary and other street crimes. The report ignores corporate and white-collar crimes such as pollution, procurement fraud, financial fraud, public corruption and occupational homicide.

The FBI does not issue a yearly *Corporate Crime in the United States* report, despite strong evidence indicating that

8

corporate crime and violence inflicts far more damage on society than all street crime combined.

Much corporate crime and violence goes undetected or unprosecuted for two reasons.

First, unlike most other criminal groups in the U.S., major corporations have enough power to define the laws under which they live.

Second, corporations have enough power to influence prosecutors not to bring criminal charges.

According to former *New York Times* reporter David Burnham, each of the past half-dozen Attorneys General have publicly committed the Justice Department to a war against white-collar crime. But as Burnham reports in his book, *Above the Law: Secret Deals, Political Fixes and Other Misadventures of the U.S. Department of Justice* (Scribner, New York, 1996) the Department doesn't walk the talk.

Burnham finds that less than half of one percent (250) of the criminal indictments (51,253) brought by the Department in 1994 involved environmental crimes, occupational safety and health crimes, and crimes involving product and consumer safety issues.

Burnham believes that corporate criminals often get away because of "unacknowledged class biases, outright political deals, poorly drafted laws and incompetent investigators" at the Justice Department.

When it comes to prosecuting white-collar crime cases, Burnham's judgment is that "the Justice Department itself could be convicted of fraud."

Despite the built-in advantages corporate criminals have in staving off judgment day, blatant acts of criminality do slip through the cracks and are prosecuted.

Forty-six executives were convicted in the "Operation-Ill-Wind" defense procurement fraud enforcement action in the early 1990s. Six major defense corporations—Cubic, Hazeltine, Loral, Sperry/Unisys, Teledyne, Whittaker—were convicted in that operation.

Exxon, International Paper, United Technologies, Weyerhauser, Pillsbury, Ashland Oil, Texaco, Nabisco and Ralston-Purina have all been convicted of environmental crimes in recent years.

Yet, despite a growing wave of corporate crime and violence lapping up over the society, if you ask the average person to name a crime, he or she most likely will say burglary, robbery, murder—not pollution, price-fixing or procurement fraud.

Television, of course, plays a major role in shaping this misperception. If the television crime shows and local news broadcasts, which now focus overwhelmingly on street crime, gave equal time to corporate crime and violence, the public perception no doubt would more accurately reflect reality.

But today, no matter what the topic—America's Most Wanted, shame or three strikes and you're out—corporate crime and violence is left out of the conversation by corporatist media elites and politicians.

This is a prescription for societal rot. As poor Americans are driven to prison in record numbers for minor drug crimes and petty burglary, wealthy Americans and their corporations elude justice for major criminal acts like pollution, corruption, and ripping off the government. Corporatist politicians like Newt Gingrich (R-Georgia) believe the time has come to "reestablish shame as means of enforcing proper behavior."

Who wouldn't agree? But let's start at the top, where the rot takes hold.

On Foreign Bribery, Justice is Out to Lunch

May 15, 1998

When it comes to prosecuting corporate crimes, Bill Clinton's Justice Department is a tiger against the smaller corporate violators, but a pussy cat when it comes to facing down the giant criminals.

The overwhelming majority of environmental corporate criminal prosecutions, for example, are brought against relatively small companies. Does this mean that smaller companies are committing more environmental crimes than bigger companies? Probably not.

It probably means, instead, that big companies have the resources to hire the well-connected corporate defense lawyers who know how to get a case dismissed, or settled as a civil or regulatory matter.

In some areas where big business dominates the field—as in the field of bribing foreign governments—the Justice Department is just out to lunch.

Lawyers handling foreign bribery cases report there has been a sharp increase in business over the past couple of years.

Homer Moyer Jr., a partner at the corporate defense law firm of Miller & Chevalier, told us last year he has had "more work in this area" in recent years "than in my previous 16 years of practice."

Why then aren't newspapers full of stories about how U.S. companies are bribing overseas?

Because the Justice Department is burying the cases.

Moyer likens his practice of defending corporations against charges of bribery to an "iceberg."

"Very little of this practice is publicly visible," Moyer said. "Many of these cases are resolved informally, without publication of consent decrees—many are just dismissed."

For years, Justice Department officials have claimed that they have large numbers of cases in the pipeline. But the pipeline gets clogged up by high-priced corporate defense attorneys.

When an enforcement action results, information that is made publicly available is often sketchy because defense counsel "negotiate what information can be released," Moyer says.

In the summer of 1974, when allegations of widespread bribery of foreign governments were being played up in the U.S. media, the Securities and Exchange Commission (SEC) offered a deal to corporate America—come clean with information about your bribes, and we'll give you some leniency. About 500 corporations disclosed questionable practices to the SEC. The Justice Department prosecuted about 100 of those cases.

The massive corruption probe forced Congress in 1976 to pass a law that outlaws U.S. companies or individuals from bribing foreign government officials.

So, has the law worked? Well, there have been very few—less than 20—criminal prosecutions under the law since it was passed more than 20 years ago.

All experts agree that the law has forced U.S. companies to change the way they do business. But have they just learned how to better conceal their wrongdoing? Or does Moyer's experience indicate that the Justice Department just isn't prosecuting cases when they should?

Only the Justice Department and defense attorneys know for sure. But a case reported by the *Cincinnati Enquirer* earlier this month will tell much about Clinton Administration and foreign bribery.

The year-long investigation by the *Enquirer* found that Chiquita Brands International Inc., the world's largest banana company, is engaged in a range of questionable business practices.

The paper found that Chiquita secretly controls dozens of supposedly independent banana companies. It does so through elaborate business structures designed to avoid restrictions on land ownership and national security laws in Central American countries. The structures also are aimed at limiting unions on its farms.

Reporters Mike Gallagher and Cameron McWhirter also reported Chiquita and its subsidiaries are engaged in pesticide practices that threaten the health of workers and nearby residents, despite an agreement with an environmental group to adhere to certain safety standards.

And the paper reported that Chiquita allegedly made business decisions in Latin America to cover up a bribery scheme involving company and subsidiary employees and helped foreign growers try to evade taxes.

The bribery incident allegedly involved paying government officials in Turbo, Colombia, to help the company's Colombian subsidiary Banadex obtain use of a large government storage facility, the paper reported.

According to the report, company records and high-level sources within the company described how, after learning of the scheme, company officials allegedly took action to hide it.

SEC investigators have issued subpoenas to Chiquita seeking documents reflecting how Chiquita obtained access to the Colombian government-owned storage space.

Chiquita issued a one page statement broadly denying the allegations in the 18-page *Enquirer* report. As for the allegations of bribery, the company issued a statement through its lawyers stating that "Chiquita's policy is not to make illegal payments to any government officials."

But sources told the *Enquirer* that two Chiquita executives have been forced to resign as a result of the brewing scandal.

The Chiquita scandal is a perfect test case for the Clinton Justice Department. Carl Lindner is well known as a big contributor to both Democrats and Republicans.

He has spent at least two nights at the Clinton White House. Campaign reform activists in Washington see Lindner, chairman of the board and CEO of Chiquita, as a CEO who has effectively bought his way into the power corridors of Washington.

The SEC is investigating these very public allegations. But where is the Justice Department? Will this be just another case that gets clogged in the pipeline?

[In June 1998, the *Cincinnati Enquirer* fired Gallagher, "renounced" the expose, and paid Chiquita $10 million to ward off a possible lawsuit. The *Enquirer*, owned by Gannett, did not challenge the accuracy of Gallagher's reporting, but did allege that Gallagher illegally raided Chiquita's e-mail system.

In September 1998, Gallagher pled guilty to two felony counts relating to the illegal interception.]

The Competitor is Our Friend, the Customer is Our Enemy

July 9, 1998

When you hear politicians blather about free markets, point them to Chicago, where three former executives of Archer Daniels Midland (ADM) are in federal court this week to face criminal charges of destroying markets.

The three former ADM executives, Michael Andreas (son of Chairman Dwayne), Terrance Wilson and Mark Whitacre have been charged with meeting with competitors to fix the prices and sales volume of the feed additive lysine.

A fourth executive, Kazutoshi Yamada, of the Ajinomoto Company, was also charged in the conspiracy to fix prices. But Yamada will not appear at the trial in Chicago to face the charges. When asked why Yamada is not being extradited, federal officials reply with a limp "no comment."

ADM and a number of other companies have already admitted their criminality and paid tens of millions of dollars in fines.

The price-fixing fits well with Chairman Dwayne's philosophy on markets. As he put it to his son Michael, "The competitor is our friend and the customer is our enemy."

"There isn't one grain of anything in the world that is sold in a free market," Dwayne told a reporter from *Mother Jones* in 1995, "Not one! The only place you see a free market is in the speeches of politicians. People who are not from the Midwest do not understand that this is a socialist country."

The extent of the price-fixing was laid out earlier this year by federal prosecutors in a little-noticed pre-trial proffer filed in Chicago.

The document quotes extensively from video and audio tapes made by former ADM-executive-turned-FBI-mole-turned-convict Whitacre. (Whitacre was convicted earlier this year of stealing millions of dollars from ADM, even though he claimed that the money was off-the-books compensation.)

The proffer is startling in its scope. It contains within its 57 pages perhaps the most concentrated proof of corporate criminality ever assembled by a federal agency.

The document, which was compiled by the Justice Department's James Griffin, argues that the agreement to fix prices was hammered out at a series of meetings, beginning with a meeting in Mexico City on June 23, 1992.

The proffer contains large excerpts from tape recordings made by Whitacre when he was a mole for the FBI. The excerpts are riddled with expletives.

According to Griffin's proffer, the government will prove at trial that at the Mexico City meeting, Wilson told other lysine producers "we are not cowboys, we should be trust(ing) and (have) competitive friendliness." Wilson points out that low lysine prices were benefitting the customers rather than the manufacturers.

After the Mexico City meeting, the companies agreed to raise the U.S. price of lysine without reaching an agreement on holding down volume. As a result, the price of lysine increased throughout the summer.

Another meeting was held in Paris in October 1992. After the Mexico City and Paris meetings, the price of lysine increased in some places, but not everywhere. The companies blamed each other for this, they began to bicker and prices dropped.

A third meeting was held in Decatur, Illinois—home to ADM—on April 30, 1993.

Prior to the Decatur meeting, Andreas and Whitacre had several strategy sessions, all of which were taped.

Wilson and Andreas contended that ADM's sole promise to the other producers in 1992 was to lower its lysine volume only if the producers were able to maintain the higher lysine prices they had agreed to.

During one such conversation, Andreas advised Whitacre: "You could just say to [Yanamoto, a Japanese competitor] look, these prices are so shitty…and you guys are so disorganized that I don't know what kind of shit you're managing."

At a March 10, 1994 meeting in Hawaii, the producers complained about each others' cheating on the fixed prices. Wilson laid out his price-fixing philosophy:

"We are gonna get manipulated by these God damn buyers…They can be smarter than us if we let them be smarter…They are not your friend. They are not my friend. And we gotta have 'em. Thank God we gotta have 'em, but they are not my friends. You are my friends. I wanna be closer to you than I am to any customer 'cause you can make us…money."

The competitor is our friend, and the customer is our enemy.

God Bless America.

[In September 1998, Mark Whitacre, Michael Andreas and Terrance Wilson were found guilty of conspiracy to fix the price of lysine, a feed additive. In denying their motion for a new trial, U.S. District Court Judge Blanche Manning wrote: "a picture is worth a thousand words, but it is nothing when compared to a videotape."]

"I'm encouraging him to stay in school and go into white-collar crime."

Blue Cross, Blue Shield, Blue Criminal

July 25, 1998

Who are the true criminals in the health insurance crisis? Try Blue Cross/Blue Shield of Illinois, for one.

Last month, the company, also known as Health Care Service Corporation (HCSC), pled guilty to eight felony counts and will pay $144 million after admitting it concealed evidence of poor performance in processing Medicare claims for the federal government.

The company, the Medicare contractor for Illinois and Michigan, also admitted obstructing justice and conspiring to obstruct federal auditors.

The company will pay $4 million in criminal fines and $140 million in a civil settlement to resolve its liability under the False Claims Act.

June Gibbs Brown is the inspector general of the Department of Health and Human Services. At a news conference at the Justice Department to announce the guilty pleas, Brown made it clear that the crimes of Blue Cross/Blue Shield of Illinois were in no way unprecedented.

"Rogue contractors have been caught cheating the program in the past and I am sure, because of the vast amount of money spent on Medicare, others will be tempted to scam the program in the future," Brown said.

By vast amount of money, Brown means $100 billion a year lost to health care fraud and abuse—and that may be a low estimate, according to experts such as Harvard's Malcolm Sparrow, who believe that the number might be as high as $300 billion to $400 billion a year.

Over the past five years, Brown's office has investigated five additional cases that have resulted in criminal or civil actions against a Medicare contractor.

In 1993, Blue Cross/Blue Shield of Florida paid $10 million to settle charges that it falsified and failed to properly screen provider claims.

In 1994, Blue Cross/Blue Shield of Massachusetts paid a $2.75 million fine to settle charges that it falsified its performance reports.

In 1995, Blue Cross/Blue Shield of Michigan paid a total of $51.6 million to settle charges that it falsified audit reports and used Medicare money to pay claims that were the responsibility of other insurers.

In 1997, Blue Shield of California pled guilty and paid $12 million in civil penalties to settle charges of falsifying documents, failing to properly process claims and destroying claims.

And in 1997, Blue Cross/Blue Shield of Massachusetts paid $700,000 to settle charges that it falsified statements related to its Medicare HMO application.

But the Blue Cross/Blue Shield of Illinois case was different at least in magnitude—$144 million in fines and damages.

And the government had to be dragged kicking and screaming into the case. If it were not for a whistleblower, Evelyn Knoob, and her attorney, Ronald Osman of Marion, Illinois, the government would never have prosecuted the case.

Knoob began working at Blue Cross/Blue Shield's Marion, Illinois facility in 1983. Over the years, she witnessed a wide range of wrongful activity, including destruction and falsification of documents.

To anyone who has ever called their health insurer only to be met by maddening tape recordings or busy signals, Knoob knows why.

The government hired Blue Cross/Blue Shield to process claims. To keep its contract, the company had to meet certain performance standards. For example, the company was supposed to answer 98 percent of the beneficiary calls within 120 seconds.

Knoob's supervisors had a way around this standard. They set up a monitor to keep track of calls. If this performance standard was about to be breached, Knoob and her colleagues were ordered to shut off the 800 line. Result: when a beneficiary called in to check on a claim, the line would be busy. A busy signal did not count as a call coming and thus did not have to be answered within 120 seconds.

In 1992, Congress held hearings about the busy signals Medicare beneficiaries were getting. The company felt the heat and changed strategies. According to Knoob, the company just stopped answering some calls. Beneficiaries would call and no one would answer.

Under the *qui tam* provisions of the False Claims Act, a private party may bring suit on behalf of the United States to recover damages resulting from the knowing submission of false claims to the government.

The party, in this case Evelyn Knoob, is entitled to receive 15 to 25 percent of the proceeds of the recovery in these cases.

That means Knoob will get anywhere from $21 million to $35 million for taking on a major corporate criminal—her employer.

In addition to bringing the False Claims Act on her behalf, Ronald Osman, Knoob's attorney, went to the Justice Department Criminal Division in Washington, D.C. to seek a criminal prosecution for the destruction of documents and creation of false documents. The Justice Department attorneys said, "No case."

Frustrated, Osman went back home and made a presentation to Chuck Grace, the U.S. attorney for the southern district of Illinois. Grace saw the crime, and assigned a number of attorneys and FBI agents to investigate the case. After two years, the company pled guilty to eight felony charges.

The government should have permanently excluded the company from ever having a contract again with Medicare. But companies the size of Blue Cross/Blue Shield do not get the death penalty—that is reserved for people only.

Accident or Corporate Manslaughter?

September 28, 1998

Let's say you've had one too many drinks.

You get into your car and drive away.

You cross the center line and hit an oncoming car. Someone in the oncoming car dies in the crash.

You didn't intend to kill that person. You are horrified that your recklessness has resulted in the death of another human being.

No matter. You will be charged with involuntary manslaughter and be sent off to prison.

Like the drunk behind the wheel, corporations generally don't intend to kill people. Yet they kill people with their reckless actions. And while in the vast majority of cases individuals will be prosecuted for involuntary manslaughter in drunk driving death cases, in the vast majority of cases corporations are not prosecuted for involuntary manslaughter when people die as a result of their recklessness.

Occasionally, organizations are charged with manslaughter. Earlier this month, a Massachusetts grand jury charged a Massachusetts Institute of Technology (MIT) fraternity with hazing and manslaughter in connection with the alcohol-related death of a student, Scott Krueger.

The Boston chapter of the Phi Gamma Delta fraternity was charged in connection with the death of Krueger, an 18- year-old MIT freshman who was found unconscious on the night of September 27, 1997 in his bedroom at the MIT frat house in Boston.

Involuntary manslaughter statutes do not require intent to kill. In California, for example, involuntary manslaughter contemplates acts which involve "a high risk of death or bodily harm," and which are committed "without due caution or circumspection." That encompasses the vast majority of corporate killings.

22

Last week, a lawyer representing Earth First! protesters called on the District Attorney in Humboldt County, California, to investigate Pacific Lumber and one of its loggers for manslaughter in connection with the death earlier this month of David Chain, a 24-year-old activist.

Chain was with a group of protesters in a forest area near Fortuna, California, trying to persuade loggers not to cut down the giant 200-year-old trees. He died when a giant tree was cut down and crushed him.

Earth First! issued a statement saying, "The loggers were aware that activists were in the woods and deliberately felled trees in their direction."

The group said that "loggers were felling trees perpendicular to the hill rather than downhill in an apparent attempt to target activists."

Pacific Lumber said the death of Chain was accidental. Pacific Lumber President John Campbell said the logging crew did not see anybody in the area and had no idea Chain was standing nearby.

"They felled a tree and apparently heard some yelling, and then the feller was cutting the tree into segments when the body was found under a limb," Campbell said.

But Richard Jay Moller, a Redway, California lawyer affiliated with Earth First!, called Pacific Lumber's contention that the loggers did not see anybody in the area an "outrageous lie."

Earth First! protesters had videotaped the protest before Chain was killed. The videotape shows the logger who later cut down the tree that killed Chain. The logger, identified only as "A.E.," is heard yelling obscenities at the group of activists.

"Get the f--- out of here," A.E. threatens. "Get outta here, otherwise I'll f---, I'll make sure I got a tree comin' this way."

A.E. is then heard telling the activists, "I wish I had my f-----' pistol. I guess I'm gonna just start packin' that mother-f----- in here. 'Cause I can only be nice so f-----' long. Go get my saw, I'm gonna start fallin' into this f-----' draw."

Moller said an independent investigation into the incident is needed because the investigative detective assigned to the case has apparently already made up his mind that the case was an "accident."

Moller called for a manslaughter prosecution against the logger, A.E., and a manslaughter investigation into the company.

Moller said that none of the witnesses believed that A.E. intended to kill Chain. "But virtually all of the witnesses believed, based on A.E.'s words and actions that day, that he was trying to scare them and was intentionally dropping trees in their direction," Moller said. "If the eyewitnesses are believed, that conduct is sufficient to constitute manslaughter."

As for Pacific Lumber [PL], Moller said that "it is critical that an independent investigator be assigned who can investigate what PL's management told its employees and loggers to do when confronted by protesters in the woods."

Moller says that California law is clear that "a corporation and high level employees can be charged and convicted of negligent homicide and involuntary manslaughter."

Most corporate criminologists agree that corporate crime and violence inflicts far more damage on society than all street crime combined. That includes killings and deaths. The time has come for the families and friends of victims to organize and demand justice and a criminal prosecution against corporations and their executives who engage in manslaughter.

The Academic Siberia
of Corporate Criminology

December 18, 1998

Want to be a corporate criminologist? Prepare for the cold winds of academic Siberia.

The American Society of Criminology held its 50th Annual Meeting recently in Washington, D.C. The program for the meeting lists 503 sessions. Fewer than ten of those sessions dealt in any way with issues of white-collar and corporate crime.

Laureen Snider, a Professor of Sociology at Queen's University in Kingston, Ontario, Canada, attended the conference. She anticipated the dearth of papers on corporate crime. The title of her paper: "The Sociology of Corporate Crime: An Obituary."

Snider's point: while corporate crime itself might be increasing around the globe, the study of corporate crime by academics has been declining rapidly over the years.

If academics study in the field of white collar crime, they study not the crimes committed by corporations, but crimes against corporations—the traditional white-collar crimes of theft, embezzlement and the like, plus newly defined white-collar crimes such as "theft of time."

Instead of focusing on criminal pollution, or the manufacture of hazardous pharmaceuticals that kill, or illegal union-busting by major corporations, the few researchers studying white collar crime are looking at how employees steal from employers.

"If, for example, you take too long on your coffee break, or if you surf the net when you 'should' be looking at something that is directly relevant to the employer's interest, you are guilty of the offense of theft of time," Snider says. "You are stealing the employer's money by taking their time."

This focus fits well with a power structure that rewards ideas supportive of the corporate domination of society, while punishing those who would question that domination.

Snider is one of the world's handful of corporate criminologists—academics who focus primarily on the study of corporate crime. She is the author of *Bad Business: Corporate Crime in Canada* (Nelson, 1993), and is the editor, along with Frank Pearce, of *Corporate Crime: Contemporary Debates* (University of Toronto Press, 1995).

Corporate criminologists like Snider tend to be found in out-of-the-way places, like Kingston, Ontario, Canada, or Adelaide, Australia, or Scranton, Pennsylvania. For some reason, the big city major universities in the United States find it inconvenient to put up with a corporate criminologist.

David Friedrichs is a corporate criminologist who has settled in at the University of Scranton in Scranton, Pennsylvania.

There, he has written *Trusted Criminals: White Collar Crime In Contemporary Society* (Wadsworth Publishing, 1996), the most comprehensive textbook on the subject.

If corporate crime and violence inflicts far more damage on society than all street crime combined, why are Snider and Friedrichs in the tiny minority of criminologists?

Friedrichs says the reasons are complex, but one reason is that there is no broad-based social movement against corporate crime.

Criminologist Jack Katz claimed that in the 1970s there was a social movement against white collar crime, but "that claim was a little overstated and perhaps premature," Friedrichs says.

"There was a growth in activity, both in terms of media coverage and interest in environmental crime and federal prosecution," he told us recently. "But there was no broad-based popular social movement."

Another reason is the fact that corporate crime is more complex and in some ways more difficult to understand than street crime.

"Corporate crime is not as easily put into sound bites as, say, a brutal rape and murder," Friedrichs says.

There are exceptions—the Exxon Valdez oil spill, for example. But it is much more complex, frustrating and expensive to have reporters investigate and report on these kinds of activities than on street crime, he points out.

"*Silence of the Lambs*, the movie about a serial killer, was a much more successful film than *Wall Street*, one of the few films that looked at white collar crime," Friedrichs says. "Serial killers cause dreadful harm to a limited number of people. But they do not represent a major threat to the society as a whole. They do not cause, over time, the kind of harm that corporations cause."

One major reason why corporate crime gets little attention from reporters, academics and government officials has little to do with complexity, and more to do with the simple reality of corporate power. Big corporations have marinated our formerly independent institutions in corporate cash and influence.

Why should reporters tackle tough issues of corporate power and crime when such a foray might lead to loss of job, income and family support? Why should academics study corporate crime when government funding sources send signals that such study is unwelcome? And why should Justice Department researchers propose to keep track of corporate crime statistics, knowing that business politicians lurk in the hallways, waiting to make life miserable?

Snider makes the obvious point that "certain ideas are much more appealing" to the powerful ruling interests.

"The idea of corporate crime is one that is simply unappealing to business elites," she says. "Ever since it was first invented by Edwin Sutherland, the concept of white collar crime, and specifically corporate crime, has been actively resisted. Corporations have certainly argued, if they have had to face up to the idea at all, that corporate executives are not criminals. We have reserved the concept of 'criminal' for people we think are different from ourselves."

The result: our prisons are filled with the poor, the minorities and the underrepresented.

In law, as in modern corporate life, you get what you pay for.

Part II
The Corporate Attack
on Democracy

Clean Food,
or Irradiated Dirty Food?

December 8, 1997

Clean food, or irradiated dirty food?

The irradiation industry is betting that consumers will settle for the latter.

Earlier this month, in response to a petition filed by Isomedix, a New Jersey radiation firm, the Food and Drug Administration (FDA) authorized the use of irradiation—a process by which food is exposed to high levels of nuclear radiation—for meat products including beef, lamb and pork. Irradiation is already permitted in the United States for poultry. Irradiation kills significant numbers of micro-organisms, such as *e. coli*.

Companies like Isomedix are hoping to ride the wave of justified public concern over outbreaks of *e. coli* and other food contaminants to overcome consumer resistance to the controversial irradiation process. Public opinion polls show three quarters of the population oppose irradiation and would refuse to eat irradiated food.

There are sound reasons underlying consumer resistance to irradiation.

First, although the FDA has approved the use of irradiation, there are serious uncertainties surrounding the safety of irradiated foods. "No long-term studies on the safety of eating irradiated beef have been conducted, and the effects on humans are unknown," notes Michael Colby, executive director of Food & Water, Inc., a Vermont-based food safety organization that is the leading opponent of food irradiation.

Second, irradiation kills "good" as well as "bad" bacteria. That means if beef becomes contaminated after irradiation, dangerous bacteria will be free to multiply without competition from harmless bacteria.

Third, irradiation fails to deal with the real food safety problem: unhealthy conditions on animal farms and in slaughterhouses and packinghouses. In the last two decades, the meat and poultry industries have become tremendously concentrated, with each sector dominated by a handful of giants like ConAgra, Cargill, Perdue and Tyson. These companies buy animals raised on "factory farms," where the animals are confined to small spaces in which bacteria can easily spread. The animals are transported to increasingly mechanized slaughterhouses and processing plants, where feces routinely spill or spray on meat, and chicken carcasses are dipped in cold water tanks contaminated with fecal material. Animals pass by workers on the corporate assembly lines at staggering speeds—often too fast for the workers to maintain proper sanitation standards, or even to identify contaminants on meat or poultry. Genuinely ensuring a safe food supply requires addressing these conditions so that animals are raised, slaughtered and processed in sanitary conditions.

There are other reasons to reject irradiation. At existing irradiation facilities (which overwhelmingly sterilize products like medical equipment rather than food), there is already a disturbing record of worker overexposure to nuclear radiation and of improper disposal of radioactive waste.

Fortunately, the FDA's approval of irradiation for beef does not mean it must be widely used. If consumers reject the technology, it will not gain a foothold in the market.

Under the innovative leadership of Food & Water, Inc., consumers so far have done exactly that. Although it has urged the government not to permit irradiation, Food & Water's emphasis has been on directing consumer pressure to food suppliers—from McDonald's to Hormel (makers of Spam) to supermarket chains—and extracting commitments that they will not sell irradiated food products. That strategy has succeeded so far, and there is good reason to believe it will continue to keep irradiated food off of supermarket shelves and out of fast-food kitchens.

The solution to the problem of dirty and contaminated meat and poultry is to clean up the beef, pork and poultry farms and the factories in which animals are slaughtered and processed—not to expose the food to nuclear radiation. That's the message consumers must send to the beef, pork and poultry companies, supermarkets, restaurant chains and other big food distributors.

Visa and the Anti-Child Support Act

February 27, 1998

Call it the Anti-Child Support Act.

It is the product of a full-throttle campaign by the credit card companies and financial services industry to rewrite U.S. bankruptcy laws.

Their goals: to make it harder to declare bankruptcy and to impose heavy burdens on debtors who do fall into bankruptcy.

More than one million Americans declare bankruptcy each year. This should not be a surprise: the credit industry sends out 2.5 billion solicitations each year; credit card advertisements urge consumers, simply, to spend; and the consumer culture encourages extravagant purchases and constantly upgrades the measure of what is an "essential" versus a "convenience." All the while, real wages have stagnated or dropped over the last 25 years for 80 percent of the population.

When people declare bankruptcy, they are required to undertake court-supervised repayment plans. During a period of three to five years, with some money set aside for essential needs like food and rent, they allocate their income to pay off their debts as best they can. At the end of the repayment period, their debts are wiped clean.

For the credit industry, of course, personal bankruptcies mean unpaid accounts. That's why the industry wants to make it harder to declare bankruptcy and more onerous to live through it.

The industry-supported "Responsible Borrower Protection Act" would force debtors to litigate their right to be in bankruptcy, and impose expensive new filing and other bureaucratic requirements—just to get into bankruptcy. Once in bankruptcy, debtors would be forced to stay in repayment plans for five to seven years. The legislation would place payment obligations for credit card debt on a par with secured debt on critically important items like a home mortgage or a car loan.

It even would place credit card debt on equal footing with child support payment obligations, says Gary Klein of the National Consumer Law Center.

In other words, debtor repayment plans could not prioritize paying off mortgages—enabling people to keep their homes—or paying back child support, over payments on overdue Visa or Mastercard accounts.

The industry spin on this draconian legislation is that it would crack down on "bankruptcies of convenience." The American Financial Services Association argues that debtors routinely file for bankruptcy to escape debts when they have the means to make payments. Bankruptcy is becoming a "financial planning tool," the Association contends.

These claims ignore some inconvenient facts: Bankruptcy debtors have an income 40 percent below the national average, for example. And the existing bankruptcy system imposes tough oversight provision on debtors, with strong civil and criminal penalties for fraud and dismissal of claims by people who can afford to pay their debts.

But the credit industry doesn't intend for facts to get in its way. It has launched a massive PR and lobbying blitz to generate public support for the Anti-Child Support Act.

Financial interests have banded together to form the National Consumer Bankruptcy Coalition. Members of the coalition poured more than $700,000 into federal candidate campaign coffers in the first half of 1997 alone.

The American Financial Services Association has hired a Dream Team of lobbyists and consultants to push the Anti-Child Support Act. Among its hires: Verner Liipfert, a law firm that is the current home of Bob Dole and Lloyd Bentsen, former treasury secretary; Timmons & Co., run by William Timmons, a top White House aide in the Nixon and Ford administrations; and former Republican National Committee Chair Haley Barbour's law firm.

The industry's big bucks and lobbyist Dream Team are all working to sabotage an institution that provides a modicum of fairness in the American economy. There is no debtor's prison in the United States; when people fall on hard times and into financial troubles from which there is no escape, we make them pay what they can—and then offer them a fresh start.

There is, of course, one serious issue of bankruptcy abuse—big corporations declaring bankruptcy to avoid liability payments for dangerous products they sold. But somehow that problem hasn't drawn the attention of the self-proclaimed advocates of "bankruptcy reform."

[The credit industry made enormous strides in 1998, with the bankruptcy bill passing the House of Representatives and nearly winning approval in the Senate. The credit industry is sure to win congressional reconsideration in 1999.]

Big Tobacco's Ruse

April 25, 1998

In the two weeks since they announced they are walking away from the negotiations over tobacco legislation, Big Tobacco has taken an unprecedented pounding.

The Clinton administration, members of Congress from both parties and the media have lined up to take potshots at the tobacco industry's shocking display of arrogance—after all, under the constitution, corporate CEOs do not have a vote in Congress, nor do they share the president's veto power.

It has been the best two weeks Big Tobacco has enjoyed in a long time.

By denouncing legislation introduced by Senator John McCain, R-Arizona, as an extremist, "big government" approach that is likely to bankrupt the industry, the tobacco merchants have succeeded in luring many into a defense of the McCain bill.

That is exactly what the industry hoped to accomplish. Big Tobacco cannot help but be happy with the McCain bill, which grants the industry a wide array of concessions and protections. But it knows the best way to generate support for the bill is to pretend to oppose it—an industry endorsement would be the kiss of death for any legislation on Capitol Hill.

Here are some of the reasons why the industry loves the McCain bill:

- A cap on liability: The McCain bill specifies that the tobacco companies cannot pay more than $6.5 billion a year in damages in civil lawsuits. This lets the tobacco companies predict future expenses—their most cherished goal, because the uncertainty surrounding litigation and the potential of huge punitive damage awards keeps tobacco stock prices depressed.

- Consumers pay, not the companies: The McCain bill requires the companies to make annual payments to the government, and to pass through the costs to consumers. All proposed tobacco legislation would, through "pass throughs" or direct taxes, raise prices for consumers, so this is not unique to the McCain bill. But it does put the lie to the industry's claim that tobacco companies may face bankruptcy under the bill. It is consumers who will pay the costs, not industry (although resultant sales volume declines may lower the companies' profits).

- An exemption from the nation's antitrust laws: The antitrust exemption will permit the companies to collude to raise prices more than required—meaning the industry may actually profit from the legislation.

In a September 1997 report, the Federal Trade Commission (FTC) concluded that similar antitrust immunity provisions in the June 20, 1997 state attorneys' general deal with the tobacco industry "may permit the industry members to discuss pricing arrangements that reach beyond the amount of a 100 percent 'pass-through' to consumers of the cost of the annual payments."

The FTC concluded that, with the June 20 settlement's antitrust immunity, "the industry may be able to increase prices and generate substantial profits."

- Payments under the McCain bill are tax deductible: That means taxpayers will cover the cost of about 40 percent of the industry's payments—even though consumers, not the companies, will really be paying the McCain bill's costs. This is an enormous opportunity for company profiteering.

- Big Tobacco's real assets shielded: The McCain bill would permit only domestic tobacco manufacturing subsidiaries to be sued. The parent companies and the foreign subsidiaries of Philip Morris and R.J. Reynolds would be completely protected from litigation. That means tobacco company victims would be denied access to most of the assets and earnings of the tobacco company conglomerates. (Philip Morris already earns more than half of its tobacco profits from overseas sales, and the portion is growing.)

- Preemption of state action: The McCain bill would prevent states from enforcing regulations stronger than those in federal legislation through civil suits against the tobacco companies. That would deter states from trying to innovate more effective regulatory measures. Other preemptive provisions in the McCain bill would also undermine community and state campaigns to control the tobacco companies.

Congress, the media and the public shouldn't be fooled by Big Tobacco's ruse. It is time to pass tough tobacco legislation—without worrying about industry's support, and without providing sweetheart deals to the Tobacco Lords. If Congress cannot pass broad legislation to control the industry, then it should pass more focused legislation—including, for example, a tax increase, affirmation of Food and Drug Administration authority to regulate tobacco and international measures—that doesn't confer any special protections and benefits on the Merchants of Death.

[The Senate went on to pass an amendment to strip the liability cap in the McCain bill. This amendment changed the industry's position to the bill to one of genuine opposition. Senate Republicans then undertook a procedural maneuver that effectively defeated the bill.]

Avoiding the Evil of Two Lessers

May 31, 1998

In the movie *Bulworth*, Warren Beatty plays Senator Jay Bulworth, a Clinton-like sell-out who is transformed into a tell-the-truth, anti-corporate activist.

The movie's message is as obvious as the headlines of today's newspapers—insurance, banking, oil and auto companies give big bucks to the major political parties, and in return get the big fix out of both ends of Pennsylvania Avenue.

Anyone not putting money into the machine—working people, poor people, inner-city blacks—won't get anything out.

The movie is great entertainment, but what is a concerned citizen to do after leaving the theater?

The people of the New Mexico's third Congressional district now have an option. Instead of voting for the lesser of the two evils, Sante Fe-area citizens who wish to put a stop to corporate control of the political system have a viable alternative—they can vote for Green Party candidate Carol Miller for Congress.

Miller, a community organizer and public health advocate, calls the corrupt two-party system "the evil of the two lessers."

Miller first ran for Congress in a special election in May 1997, when the seat was vacated by Bill Richardson, who was appointed to be head of the U.S. mission to the United Nations.

She garnered an impressive 17 percent of the vote, effectively knocking out the machine Democratic, Eric Serna (40 percent), and electing a right-wing Republican, Bill Redmond (43 percent).

Citizens activists forced to confront corporate crime and violence in their community increasingly see that Big Business dominates both major parties.

The question has been how to take back the government from the corporations. Citizen activists have answered with setting up hundreds of public interest and community groups in

Washington and around the country to pressure politicians into doing the right thing.

By running candidates for political office, the Greens are saying, in effect, that the failed public interest model is not enough, that it is time to become overtly political.

Instead of pressuring politicians from the outside, it is time to get down and dirty and engage the political process directly, and by so doing, recapture our government from the corporations.

Miller's political history is a case in point. For more than three decades, Miller has worked as a public health activist. She was turned off from Democratic Party politics after a stint with the Clinton White House, where she was invited to work on health care reform.

She was invited to join Hillary Clinton's health care reform project and agreed to go to the White House in an effort to convince the Clinton administration to implement a single-payer, Canadian-style health care system.

After watching the Clinton administration cave to insurance interests and reject single payer, Miller left Washington in disgust and returned to New Mexico with an eye toward confronting the Democrats and Republicans directly at the voting booth.

This year, she will face the incumbent Congressman Redmond and probably Tom Udall, New Mexico's attorney general. (A recent *Sante Fe New Mexican* poll shows Udall leading Serna in the upcoming Democratic primary by 35 to 26 percent with 19 percent undecided.)

Udall is the son of Stewart Udall, the former member of Congress from Arizona and interior secretary. The Udalls have a reputation of being liberal environmentalists, but Tom has been wavering on environmental issues in New Mexico, including the proposed nuclear waste dump outside of Carlsbad, known as the Waste Isolation Pilot Plant (WIPP).

Miller says WIPP, which will involve the transportation of nuclear waste to New Mexico from 22 states, can never be made safe.

She is also critical of Udall for not aggressively investigating the oil companies, as Udall has promised to do, for the price-fixing of gasoline.

Miller is the only major candidate in the race raising the issues of corporate control of her district—nuclear waste burial, price-fixing by gasoline companies, alleged pollution at Intel's facility in Rio Rancho and nuclear safety issues at the government's nuclear bomb facility just outside Sante Fe at Los Alamos.

She believes she can win the election, because the 17 percent she received in 1997 gave her increased name recognition and credibility, because of Redmond's corporatist record and because she believes both Serna and Udall have opened themselves up to criticism as wishy-washy corporatist Democrats.

How does Miller feel about Green Party's track record of being the spoiler and electing Republicans?

"We have to get out there and run," Miller says. "If some Democrats lose, that's the price you pay."

[Tom Udall spent $1.6 million on the election, to Carol Miller's $25,000. Udall won with 53 percent of the vote to Bill Redmond's 43 percent and Miller's 4 percent.]

The Citibank–Travelers Steamroller

October 5, 1998

Civil disobedience works.

That's the effective mantra of two unlikely sources, Citicorp and Travelers Group, two giant multinationals who have put to shame the civil disobedience records of radical environmentalists, old-line civil rights activists and faith-based pacificists.

In April, Citicorp and Travelers announced plans to undertake a merger that was prohibited by law. Although federal law bans corporate marriages between banking and insurance companies, the two companies took advantage of a loophole in the law that permits a two-year review by the Federal Reserve—with an up-to-three-year extension—before such mergers must be disallowed.

Citicorp had long opposed efforts to roll back the Bank Holding Company Act provisions that bar banking, securities and insurance firms from owning each other, but following the merger announcement, it changed its position overnight.

Operating under the misleading banner of "financial modernization," John Reed, CEO of Citicorp, and Sanford Weill, CEO of Travelers, quickly became the leaders of the corporate crusade to permit common ownership of banks, insurance companies and securities companies.

Their legislative vehicle is known as HR 10. With bickering among insurance agents and bankers over relatively unimportant issues resolved, momentum is now building to speed the legislation through the Senate. The House of Representatives passed a different version in May, but Speaker Newt Gingrich has indicated the House will rubber stamp any banking bill that emerges from the Senate.

Much more is at stake in HR 10 than the parochial interests of Citicorp and Travelers. HR 10 is an invitation for a new round of financial industry mergers. It is also likely to spur a new assault on the wall separating banking and commerce.

Although banks are not permitted to own commercial firms, HR 10 contains a grandfather clause that permits insurance and securities firms to maintain their existing commercial and industrial holdings, even after merging with banks. That breach in the barrier between banking and commerce is likely to quickly expand and destroy the wall altogether.

At a time when the financial world is in serious turmoil, with international loans going bad and the bailout of the Long Term Capital hedge fund perhaps foreshadowing a new area of widespread financial weaknesses, HR 10 introduces more uncertainty into the system at the worst possible moment.

At the same time, HR 10 does nothing to coordinate the banking and insurance regulatory system—now scattered among six federal agencies and the states—which is sure to be overwhelmed by the rash of megamergers and new gigantic financial institutions.

And when financial regulations are weak, imprudent behavior is almost sure to follow. In other words, if HR 10 is adopted, expect to see lots of bad loans, bad investment decisions, teetering banks and tottering insurance companies—and a series of massive financial bailouts of new conglomerates judged "too big to fail." The concern will be that permitting, say, an insurance company to fail would endanger the health of its conglomerate parent, which would in turn threaten a crisis of confidence in the entire financial sector.

HR 10 also raises serious concerns about the provision of consumer services: big banks tend to charge much more for consumer services; the bill fails to require banks to provide reasonable cost checking and savings accounts to the poor; and the legislation not only fails to extend but weakens the Community Reinvestment Act, which imposes obligations on banks to make loans in low-income neighborhoods.

All of these risks and costs are justified as necessitated by the imperatives of "modernization" and "globalization." But these amorphous terms have no concrete meaning. The only gain promised to consumers is "one-stop shopping" for financial services, a dubious benefit at best.

There is still time to stop HR 10. Some members of the Senate may be ready to stand up for consumer and taxpayer interests and block movement of the bill. And the Clinton administration, which favors the essential provisions of the legislation, is threatening a veto over regulatory turf fights that are important, but orders of magnitude less consequential than the core concerns about economic concentration.

Civil disobedience can be a compelling way to speak truth to power. But the Citicorp–Travelers merger and HR 10 are more about power riding roughshod over truth.

[With time running out in the 1998 legislative session, the turf fight between the Clinton administration and Alan Greenspan's Federal Reserve over which agency would be given authority to regulate new financial conglomerates led Senate Majority Leader Trent Lott to pull HR 10 from consideration. The financial industry is seeking passage of a nearly identical bill in 1999.]

Boom and Bailout

October 9, 1998

So, you are in charge of investing $4.5 billion.

You hire two Nobel Prize economists to generate computer models on how to invest in world bond markets.

You borrow billions more and put down a big chunk on a bet that differentials between certain world bond prices, out of kilter because of the global crunch, will revert to their historic levels. They don't. You lose $4 billion.

Your clients—who needed to pony up $10 million just to be in your hedge fund—are apoplectic. They call. They want to know what the hell is going on.

Boom and bust?

Don't be silly. That's capitalism for the small guy. If we go to Atlantic City or Las Vegas, make a bundle and then lose it all, then that's boom and bust. For the rich, it's boom and bailout.

So, you're John Meriwether, the bond trader who was forced to leave Salomon Brothers in 1991 after a trading scandal.

And you leave to start Long Term Capital. And for the first couple of years, you are making 30 percent return on investment for your millionaire friends. And they are loving it. And then you lose the $4 billion.

Who do you call?

The Federal Reserve Board—bailout central.

So it was that on a late August day, New York Federal Reserve Bank President William J. McDonough received a phone call from Meriwether and bailout fix-it man supreme David W. Mullins Jr., the architect of the bailout of the savings and loans under President Bush.

Big institutional investors in the hedge fund—Merrill Lynch & Co., Goldman Sachs & Co., Bear, Stearns & Co. and Bankers Trust Corp.—were also calling begging for a bailout.

These companies were of course seeking to save their own skin. But McDonough put forth the official spin before a House of Representatives Committee earlier this month.

"Everyone I spoke to that day volunteered concern about the serious effect the deteriorating situation of Long Term Capital could have on world markets," McDonough said.

Ah yes, world markets. And so McDonough calls Fed Chair Alan Greenspan and Treasury Secretary Robert Rubin and a bailout is arranged.

Former Lehman Brothers partner and current financial columnist Michael Thomas is right—it was improper for the Federal Reserve to arrange a private bailout. If Merrill Lynch and Goldman Sachs want to protect their behinds by arranging for a private bailout, fine. But the Fed should have stayed out of it.

Or, as former Fed Chair Paul Volcker asked in a speech, "Why should the weight of the Federal Government be brought to bear to help out a private investor?"

"Capitalists now all want it one way," Thomas says. "They want to do whatever the hell they feel like, but let someone else pay. It's called privatizing the profits and socializing the risks."

Hedge funds, which make complicated financial bets with millions and billions of borrowed dollars and are almost totally unregulated, do indeed pose risks to the economy. Because of the nature of their gambles, they can lose huge amounts of money, leaving investors holding the bag (absent a bailout). Even worse, they leverage borrowed money to exert extraordinary influence over markets, and cause serious problems when they overreact en masse to new fads. (That's a big part of why the value of the dollar has plunged recently, for example.)

But these are reasons why hedge funds must be subjected to regulatory discipline—not an argument for why high rollers deserve government-orchestrated bailouts.

With the global financial system in frenetic disarray, Long Term Capital is not likely to be the last financial player to go bust. If the government is not able to act quickly to rein in hedge funds and other unbridled financial activities, it should at least declare that no bailouts will follow in the wake of Long Term Capital. Each bailout makes the next one more likely, as investors are given implicit assurances that they will not have to face the down side of risky bets gone bad.

The gamblers in Atlantic City don't get this kind of treatment. Neither should those on Wall Street.

An Allergy to Democracy

October 16, 1998

If autumn is the most beautiful time in New England, it is the most dangerous in Washington, D.C.—at least every two years, when members of Congress are rushing to get home to attend to election races.

In the frenzy of backroom deal-making that constitutes the law-making process at the end of election-year congressional sessions, corporations line up to add favored special-interest provisions (known as "riders") to spending bills.

The process was particularly murky and corrupt this year. With Congress unable to reach agreement on more than half the spending bills it must pass to enable the government to function, it decided to wrap them into a single "omnibus" bill, the terms of which were negotiated in secret among a few members of Congress and the White House.

Jumping to the front of the corporate handout line was Schering-Plough, the maker of the popular allergy drug Claritin, and hardly a company in need. (You know Claritin: it's the one advertised pervasively on television, in magazines and on billboards with pictures of meadows and "blue skies.")

Following Schering-Plough maneuvers that won two separate patent extensions on the drug, the Claritin patent is now set to run out in the year 2002. That will enable generic producers to begin making the drug, which they will sell at prices far less than Schering-Plough charges.

Since generic products typically sell at prices 30 to 60 percent less than brand-name pharmaceuticals, consumers can expect to reap big savings. With 1997 sales of Claritin totaling $869 million, the 30-to-60 percent discount rate would save consumers between $261 million to $521 million a year.

Those savings, however, will come at the expense of Schering-Plough's monopoly profits.

What's a multi-billion dollar company to do?

Well, when you are a corporation of that size and face problems, you call up your senator. So the New Jersey-based company turned to Senator Frank Lautenberg, D-New Jersey, and asked him to insert a provision in the omnibus appropriations bill which would allow pharmaceutical manufacturers to petition the Patent and Trade Office to extend the patents of a small class of drugs (seven in total). Claritin is by far the best-selling among those seven drugs.

Schering-Plough spends more than $2 million a year on lobbyists. In recent years, those lobbyists have diligently, but so far unsuccessfully, lobbied for adoption of the patent-extension provision. With the secrecy and chaos surrounding the drafting of the omnibus appropriations bill, they thought they had finally found the opportunity for which they had been waiting.

Unfortunately for Schering-Plough, the patent-extension scheme was discovered. The consumer group Public Citizen and the generic manufacturer trade association began publicizing and lobbying against the proposed Claritin rip-off.

"Claritin's manufacturer, Schering-Plough, had 1997 profits of $1.2 billion, a 17 percent profit rate," says Dr. Sidney Wolfe, director of Public Citizen's Health Research Group. "It is unconscionable that seniors on fixed incomes could be required to pay hundreds of dollars more a year to further boost the company's bottom line." By way of example, Wolfe estimated that Schering-Plough's proposed private Claritin "tax" would cost consumers of the pill in the Washington, D.C. area $246 to $492 a year.

With Public Citizen and the generic makers shining the light of day on the Claritin scam, the plan withered. The final omnibus appropriations bill is not expected to include the Schering-Plough welfare provision.

And that's why big corporations have an allergy to openness and democracy.

Stacking the Decks

October 30, 1998

If there is one thing gambling operators know, it is to make sure the odds always favor the house.

Unfortunately, big gambling interests are now translating this business approach into a political strategy.

With massive campaign contributions, they are trying to stack the political deck in favor of legalized gambling expansion. Gambling interests have contributed more than a million dollars to federal candidates and to the Republican Party in the 1997–1998 election cycle.

But the gamblers are making their biggest investments in state races:

- In South Carolina, video gaming interests are leading the charge to dump incumbent Republican Governor David Beasley, a gambling critic. Led by Fred Collins, who has just under 4,000 licenses for video poker machines in the state, the video poker lobby has contributed more than $400,000 to Beasley's opponent, Democrat Jim Hodges, and spent huge additional sums on independent attack ads.

- In Maryland, slot machine interests have donated more than $500,000 to the Republican National Committee. Incumbent Governor Parris Glendening has blocked the introduction of slots at racetracks and other sites around the state. Hilton Hotels, which owns a Maryland race track and Bally's Entertainment, gave $250,000 to the Republican National Committee shortly before the RNC began running a new series of attack ads against Glendening.

- In Missouri, the casino industry has poured $8 million into a referendum campaign to support a measure that would permit "riverboat" gambling facilities to operate on "artificial spaces that contain water and that are within 1,000 feet" of a river. If the measure fails, 11 of 15 casinos would lose their permits to run "games of chance," including slot machines.

The electoral battles come at a critical juncture for the gambling industry. Over the last dozen years or so, downtrodden and deindustrialized states and communities across the United States have decided to place their bets on gambling-led economic development, legalizing forms of gambling ranging from video poker to full-fledged casinos.

Casinos have rushed to legitimize their newfound social acceptance, seeking to replace the term "gambling" with "gaming" or "gaming-entertainment," terms meant to equate gambling with other forms of entertainment and to portray gambling as an activity with which the whole family can be associated. In June 1995, fourteen large gambling operations created the American Gaming Association, which is now run by Frank Fahrenkopf, former chair of the Republican National Committee.

But in recent years, opponents of the industry have organized broad-based populist coalitions. These conservative-liberal coalitions have been extraordinarily successful, registering more than two dozen wins in gambling expansion referenda.

While many gambling opponents are motivated by its perceived immorality, the overriding argument against gambling, says Tom Grey, field coordinator for the National Coalition Against Legalized Gambling, is that gambling is "not good economics, not good politics and not good for the quality of life."

While casino and other gambling interests allege that gambling creates jobs, opponents retort that money spent on gambling is merely diverted from other forms of entertainment, meaning there is no net job creation. Unlike other forms of entertainment, however, gambling creates serious "externalities."

More than 5 percent of gamblers may become addicted where gambling is prevalent. Problem gamblers impose large social costs, through running up debts, committing crime—including not just theft and embezzlement, but child and spousal abuse—and taxing the criminal justice system. Robert Goodland, author of *The Luck Business*, estimates the cost of each problem gambler at well over $10,000.

Legalized gambling also works as a tax on the poor. Poorer people gamble with proportionally higher stakes than wealthier gamblers.

If the political game weren't rigged, the growing grassroots movement against gambling would already have won, at least, an effective moratorium on legalized gambling expansion. But when citizen interests face off against concentrated corporate power, it is never safe to bet against the corporations.

[The gambling industry hit a mini-jackpot in the 1998 elections. Democrat Jim Hodges won the South Carolina gubernatorial election, due in large part to efforts on his behalf by video poker interests. The Missouri referendum on riverboat gambling passed. The industry suffered a minor setback in Maryland, where Parris Glendening was able to win reelection despite the strong gambling industry support for his opponent.]

Part III
The Global Hunt for
Mega-Profits

Sanctioning Burma,
Sanctioning the United States

December 23, 1997

Can the European Union (EU) and Japan force U.S. states to do business with those who do business with dictators?

Yes, allege the EU and Japan, making a powerful argument under the rules of the World Trade Organization (WTO).

Last week, Japan joined the European Union in challenging a 1996 Massachusetts law preventing state agencies from purchasing goods or services from companies that do business with Burma. Burma is currently ruled by a brutal junta, known as the SLORC (the State Law and Order Restoration Council), which has killed thousands of Burmese and annulled the election in which Nobel Prize winner Aung San Suu Kyi was elected president.

Earlier this year, the EU sent a formal diplomatic submission to the U.S. State Department arguing that the Massachusetts selective purchasing law violates the WTO Government Procurement Agreement. Japan has since seconded the EU objection.

The EU says the Massachusetts law violates the WTO agreement because it "allows the award of contracts to be based on political instead of economic considerations," such as price and quality.

The EU and Japan have now entered formal negotiations with the United States in an effort to convince the federal government to force Massachusetts to repeal its law.

If the law is not changed, the EU and Japan are on course to bring a formal case against the United States in the WTO, where a panel of foreign trade bureaucrats would be empowered to decide whether the Massachusetts law complies with WTO rules. If the United States lost, the federal government would have to force Massachusetts to change its law, or accept sanctions or fines.

The European Union itself has implemented sanctions against Burma, recently lifting tariff preferences for the country under the Generalized System of Preferences. Nonetheless, the EU argues that the means Massachusetts has chosen to sanction Burma are illegal, even though they apply equally to U.S. and foreign corporations.

The Massachusetts law "is a major breach of an international code to which the state of Massachusetts has agreed and to which the United States has agreed," says Ella Krucoff, an EU spokesperson in Washington, D.C. "We don't believe this kind of action is fair to the trade and investment community."

Condemned by the EU, selective purchasing laws have been endorsed by Aung San Suu Kyi. It is easy to see why. The Massachusetts law has significantly influenced corporate decisions to deal with the Burmese generals. Since its passage, Apple Computer, Eastman Kodak, Philips Electronics and Hewlett-Packard have pulled out of Burma, moves attributed in significant part to the Massachusetts law and the possibility that other states and cities will soon follow suit.

"If the World Trade Organization agreements had been successfully used against South Africa selective purchasing laws, then Nelson Mandela might still be in prison," says Simon Billenness, a leading campaigner for the Massachusetts selective purchasing law.

The EU/Japan challenge to the Massachusetts law is intended to chill other states' consideration of selective purchasing laws against Burma or other countries ruled by heinous regimes. Connecticut, Texas, North Carolina, Vermont and California are among the states now considering selective purchasing laws against Burma.

Not coincidentally, the EU challenge comes as U.S. businesses have mounted a major campaign against unilateral trade sanctions of all sorts by U.S. states and the federal government. Hundreds of large corporations have together set up USA*Engage, a business coalition to lobby against trade sanctions.

Decisions about selective purchasing laws and related matters belong in state houses and city halls, not in closed tribunals in Geneva. Should the European Union and Japan be able to force Massachusetts to deal with those who deal with the Burmese dictators? Surely not. To preserve Massachusetts and other states' freedom of action, the United States should pull out of the WTO.

[In 1998, the European formally challenged Massachusetts' Burma sanctions law at the World Trade Organization. But the WTO may never decide the case, given the potential success of a U.S. business suit against the law in U.S. courts (see "When the People Speak, the Corporations Squeak").]

The Bailout of Banks

January 14, 1998

Oh, to be a big American banker.

Make lots of money, with little or no risk.

Thanks to Secretary of Treasury Robert Rubin and the International Monetary Fund (IMF), those are the terms upon which big U.S. banks effectively operate.

The Asian financial crisis has many causes and consequences, but imprudent loans by U.S. banks to businesses in South Korea and elsewhere are an important part of the story. Those loans helped create the crisis by supporting unsound investments and creating repayment obligations that Korean enterprises were unable to satisfy, thus undermining financial market confidence in the South Korean economy.

By all rights, one of the consequences of the crisis should be that the banks which made bad loans in South Korea and elsewhere in Asia should have to swallow hard and eat their losses. The amounts at stake are not insignificant: U.S. banks' exposure in South Korea is estimated to total more than $20 billion. BankAmerica alone reportedly has more than $3 billion in outstanding loans to South Korean firms, and Citicorp more than $2 billion.

Now, due to the taxpayer-backed bailout engineered by Rubin and the IMF, it does not appear that BankAmerica, Citicorp or the other major banks with outstanding loans to South Korea—J.P. Morgan, Bankers Trust, the Bank of New York and Chase Manhattan—will lose a penny.

The Rubin/IMF plan is funnelling tens of billions of dollars of new, public sector loans to South Korea. Much of that money will go to pay back the big U.S. banks. In exchange for this bailout, the banks have agreed only to stretch out the payment period.

Not only is the Rubin/IMF scheme an unconscionable bailout of the big banks which were complicit in the South Korean financial debacle, it is certain to create what is known as a "moral hazard." Simply put, that means we can expect to see more reckless lending by the big banks, which—following the Mexican and now South Korean bailouts—know they can count on public subsidies if their loans go bad.

There is more, for the Rubin/IMF program does much more than bail out the banks. In exchange for instilling liquidity into the South Korean economy, it imposes a series of onerous conditions on South Korea, many of which have no connection to South Korea's financial crisis—and are actually likely to exacerbate the crisis and further weaken the South Korean economy. Among these conditions are contractionary fiscal and monetary measures which will throw tens of thousands of South Korean workers out of work. These and other austerity measures will inflict enormous suffering—much of it avoidable—on South Koreans. And with the domestic market shrinking, and Korean wages falling as a result of the austerity measures, look for Korean exports to increase—and for commensurate pressure on wages and jobs in the United States. None of this foreseeable pain will be shared by the U.S. banks.

Another, particularly notable, set of counterproductive conditions imposed by the IMF and Rubin will require South Korea to open up its economy to foreign investors. Rubin has specifically and successfully pressured Korea to open up its financial sector.

Translation: the very American banks which contributed to South Korea's crisis now stand to buy up lucrative sectors of the South Korean economy at fire-sale prices.

Virtually riskless lending, taxpayer bailouts, government-ordered bargain-basement sales of foreign enterprises' assets—these are the privileges of the megabanks.

Most of what Rubin—operating without any congressional authorization—and the IMF have done is done and unfixable, barring a sudden reversal of allegiances by the Treasury Secretary and the IMF. But it is possible to draw the line with the Korean/BankAmerica bailout.

Two steps are crucial: First, Congress must pass legislation which prohibits the Treasury Secretary from allocating large amounts of taxpayer money without prior congressional approval. Second, Congress should refuse to authorize additional funds for the IMF (now seeking nearly $20 billion in new monies), which mechanically imposes crushing austerity measures on all of its borrowers but is sure to tread ever so softly where big bankers are concerned.

[Legislation to limit the ability of the Treasury Secretary to use large amounts of taxpayer money for financial bailouts in international markets, introduced by Representative Bernie Sanders, an independent from Vermont, failed to pass the House of Representatives in a close vote. And, in a last minute "omnibus" funding bill at the end of the 1998 legislative session, Congress appropriated $18 billion to the IMF.]

Truly Retiring the Marlboro Man

March 10, 1998

Imagine you were Geoffrey Bible, CEO of Philip Morris. You would have two overriding goals: First, to limit your liability from lawsuits in the United States. Second, to make sure nothing interfered with your plans to expand massively abroad.

In the deal the tobacco industry concluded with 40 state attorneys general last June, Bible and the other tobacco executives achieved both of these aims. The deal gave the industry effective immunity from lawsuits by precluding class action lawsuits, preventing punitive damage awards to those who sue the industry and setting an annual cap that would assure the industry was required to pay no more than $5 billion a year to victims who successfully sued the tobacco companies. And it did absolutely nothing to curb Big Tobacco's overseas expansion.

The exclusion of international issues from the deal was not a simple oversight. When some of the attorney general negotiators raised it, Big Tobacco dismissed it out of hand. In the face of industry obstinacy, the attorneys general quickly capitulated.

In fact, the June deal would actually make matters worse internationally. The deal specifically denied the Food and Drug Administration authority to regulate tobacco exports. It stated that, in the event of bankruptcy, the tobacco companies would be able to segment profits from overseas sales from their domestic bankruptcy payment obligations. And it denied foreign victims of the U.S. tobacco companies their limited right of access to U.S. courts. Unfortunately, many of these flaws have been replicated in several of the pending tobacco bills under congressional consideration.

What happens to the Tobacco Lords' foreign operations is of tremendous importance both to the health of the tobacco companies and, more importantly, to the health of millions of people around the world.

Philip Morris and R.J. Reynolds sell approximately two-thirds of their cigarettes overseas, and make nearly half their profits on foreign sales.

These sales do not just displace other companies' sales. U.S. tobacco companies' marketing strategies create more smokers. After South Korea opened its market to U.S. companies in 1988, for example, smoking rates among male Korean teens rose from 18.4 percent to 29.8 percent in a single year. The rate among female teens more than quintupled, from 1.6 percent to 8.7 percent.

With smoking rates rising in the Third World due to rising incomes, corporate tobacco pushing and other causes, the World Health Organization predicts tobacco-related deaths worldwide will rise from 3 million to 10 million by the 2020s, with 70 percent of those fatalities in the developing world.

There is, however, reason to be hopeful that Geoffrey Bible and his associates will not succeed in their scheme to protect industry profits and continue uninhibitedly addicting millions around the globe. Yet even as prospects for tobacco company special protections are fading on Capitol Hill, a group of legislators have crafted an international tobacco control package that would begin to address Big Tobacco's international misconduct.

In late February, Senators Richard Durbin, D-Illinois, Frank Lautenberg, D-New Jersey, Paul Wellstone, D-Minnesota, and Ron Wyden, D-Oregon, joined with Representatives Lloyd Doggett, D-Texas, and Frank Pallone, D-New Jersey, to announce a legislative initiative that would require U.S. tobacco companies to adhere to at least as stringent marketing and labeling standards overseas as domestically.

Other provisions of the package would: prohibit the U.S. government from promoting U.S. tobacco interests in foreign markets; impose tough anti-smuggling provisions on tobacco products; and support governmental and non-governmental tobacco control efforts, including television counteradvertisements urging people not to smoke, in developing countries and in Eastern Europe and the former Soviet Union.

Some Republican support for at least portions of the package is expected to be forthcoming.

Imagine that instead of Geoffrey Bible, you were a parent of a 15-year-old in Beijing or Seoul, in Nairobi or Sao Paulo, in Moscow or Kiev. In recent years, the U.S. tobacco companies have begun introducing a host of slick marketing techniques—free cigarette giveaways, sponsorships of rock concerts and sports events, discotheque dance nights, promotional T-shirts, hats and other attire, and many others—that make smoking seem cool, hip, sophisticated and very, very American. Smoking rates among teens are rising. Wouldn't you hope that the U.S. government would at least ensure that U.S. tobacco companies not expose your child to deceptive marketing strategies that are outlawed or about to be banned in the United States?

[Some version of the international tobacco control legislative package appeared in every major tobacco bill introduced in 1998, but none of those bills ultimately passed.]

When the People Speak, the Corporations Squeak

May 10, 1998

When the people speak, the corporations squeak.

Having learned from the South African divestment movement that local actions can help stop egregious human rights abuses and bring democracy to countries around the world, citizens across the United States are increasingly mobilizing in support of state and local sanctions against countries such as Burma, Nigeria and Indonesia, all of which are ruled by brutal dictatorships.

These sanctions typically leverage the power of government agencies as consumer, using "selective purchasing" laws to bar the government from doing business with companies that do business in the targeted country. Massachusetts and more than a dozen cities have adopted such laws.

The idea is to encourage corporations to stop doing business in dictatorial countries, on the theory that income from their investments helps prop up autocratic regimes. The South African example—where state and local sanctions, along with university and private divestment campaigns and national sanctions unquestionably helped speed the end of apartheid—lends strong credence to the theory.

Facing a rising tide of state and local sanctions, Big Business has banded together into an outfit called USA*Engage to defeat and roll back grassroots efforts to influence where multinationals do business. USA*Engage has more than 600 members, including Aetna, Bechtel, Cargill, Caterpillar, Exxon, Mobil, Monsanto, Pepsi, TRW and United Technologies.

In March, the state of Maryland was on the verge of enacting a selective purchasing law that targeted Nigeria. Nigeria is ruled by a military government that feeds on oil money (provided by companies like Shell and Mobil) and drug money. The government annulled a democratic election held in 1993, has jailed the victor in that election, allegedly killed his wife, executed Ken Saro-Wiwa, a leader of the Ogoni people, murdered and tortured thousands of citizens and jailed the nation's trade union leadership. All in all, Nigeria is an excellent candidate for sanctions.

But not in the eyes of Big Business. It launched a furious campaign to defeat the selective purchasing proposal, arguing that sanctions are ineffective, unfairly disadvantage U.S. companies and undermine federal authority to make foreign policy. At the last minute, the Clinton administration intervened, saying Maryland's proposed law would violate U.S. trade treaty obligations. This tipped the balance against the bill. Big Business's lobbyists were smiling when they left Maryland.

Now, the same band of companies is seeking to roll back Massachusetts's selective purchasing law which targets Burma, another military dictatorship which has killed thousands, jailed the nation's rightfully elected leader and thrives on oil money (especially from Unocal) and drug money.

Late last month, the National Foreign Trade Council, another business coalition, with 550 U.S. manufacturing company members, filed suit against Massachusetts, claiming the state's selective purchasing law infringes on the federal government's foreign policy-making power.

The lawsuit faces significant hurdles. It is not clear that the Trade Council has legal standing to bring the suit, nor that local and state sanctions interfere with federal powers in any constitutionally significant way.

But while the suit winds its way through the federal courts, it sends a powerful, chilling message to state and local officials considering responding to citizen campaigns to adopt sanctions. The message: states and localities that seek to enact selective purchasing proposals will face unremitting pressure from politically powerful multinational corporations. They should expect massive corporate lobbying campaigns, threats of lawsuits, pressure from a federal government which is choosing to ally itself with business interests on sanctions and the threat of suit at the World Trade Organization and other trade bodies (indeed, the European Union and Japan have both threatened to call for the formation of penalty-wielding WTO dispute settlement panels to rule against Massachusetts's Burma law).

The purpose of this corporate campaign of intimidation is clear: while multinationals may or may not prefer to do business with dictators, they certainly do not want citizens interfering with their commercial operations in authoritarian countries—even if those operations help prop up dictatorships.

At root, the suit over Massachusetts's Burma law is a clash between corporate internationalism and citizen internationalism.

The outcome of the clash will have huge consequences. As citizen internationalists like to point out, if the corporate internationalists' argument had prevailed in the case of South Africa, Nelson Mandela might still be in jail.

[In November 1998, a federal court ruled on behalf of the National Foreign Trade Council, finding the Massachusetts law unconstitutional. That ruling is under appeal as this book goes to press.]

The Suharto–U.S.
Corporate Connection

May 26, 1998

The sudden exit of Suharto from the Indonesian presidency has cast the international spotlight on the crony capitalism that enabled Suharto and his family to amass a fortune estimated to be on the order of $40 billion. Bribery and graft, sweetheart government contracts, government-protected monopolies and a host of other schemes made the Suharto family and a small coterie of close friends into billionaires.

Much less noted are the ways in which the Suharto regime facilitated super-profitmaking by foreign multinational corporations which eagerly accepted benefits and protections from Suharto's brutal dictatorship.

Foreign multinational corporations benefited from the twin pillars of the Suharto economic program: unsustainable extraction of Indonesia's rich natural resources and unabashed exploitation of poor, unorganized Indonesian workers.

Consider the New Orleans-based Freeport McMoRan, which operates the world's largest gold mine and third largest copper mine in Irian Jaya, the Indonesia side of the island of New Guinea.

The company has ripped the top 500 feet off Puncuk Jaya Mountain, sifting through the dirt for copper and gold. After crushing the ore, mixing it with water and dousing the mix with chemicals to bring the metals to the surface, Freeport dumps the resultant waste rock—more than 100,000 tons a day—into mountain rivers.

Those rivers are the lifeblood of downstream communities of thousands of indigenous people. Environmentalists and the indigenous people themselves charge the rock waste has poisoned the water, killing fish and the riverside forest and making massive floodplains inhospitable to crops. Freeport denies the charges.

But the Amungme and Komoro peoples are angry enough to have organized ongoing protests. The Indonesian military has met those protests with an iron fist, beating, torturing and killing many of the indigenous protesters. Freeport denies any responsibility for the military's human rights abuses of the protesters, and also denies charges that it has assisted the repression.

The Freeport-McMoRan controversy is typical of resource controversies in Indonesia, with local communities fighting against pillage of their resources and pollution of their lands and water by big national and multinational mining, oil and timber companies operating with the protection of the Indonesian military.

Or consider Nike, which is emblematic of the labor-intensive manufacturers that have located production (directly or through subcontractors) in Indonesia.

Nike subcontractors in Indonesia have two great advantages. First, wage levels in Indonesia are extremely low (though not as low as China and Vietnam). The minimum wage, which the government acknowledged to be below a "living wage," was set at $2.46 a day in 1997. With the collapse of the Indonesian currency, the rupiah, Indonesians' real earning power has dropped by about three-quarters. Stated otherwise, the real wage cost to Nike and other foreign investors has dropped by 75 percent. Under pressure, Nike agreed to nudge up workers' wages, but not to pre-financial-collapse levels.

The second benefit conferred on foreign investors like Nike is vicious repression of workers' attempts to organize. Under Suharto, Indonesia allowed only one official trade union federation. Workers' attempts at independent organizing were routinely quashed, with rival union meetings broken up by security forces and strikers facing threats and firings. Muchtar Pakpahan, the founder and leader of an unauthorized, independent labor federation, languished in an Indonesian jail until he was freed earlier this week.

Against this backdrop, in moving displays of courage, Nike's workers—most of them girls and young women—

walked out twice in 1997. Still, conditions in Nike subcontractor factories remain dismal.

Protests against both Nike and Freeport McMoRan in Suharto's Indonesia helped spark solidarity campaigns in the United States. The higher-profile campaign against Nike has recently scored an important victory, as Nike CEO Phil Knight announced the company would require subcontractors to permit independent monitoring of their shops and to enforce U.S. occupational safety standards.

Even if Nike carries out these promises in good faith, much more remains to be done: Knight did not announce an upgrading of wages nor explain how workers' right to organize would be guaranteed in countries that do not respect basic labor rights.

The ouster of Suharto should further empower grassroots and labor activists in Indonesia, which should in turn embolden allies in the United States and elsewhere in the industrialized world to turn up the heat on corporations doing business in Indonesia.

But the overthrow of one of Asia's most brutal dictators should also be a moment of pause for Americans, a time to contemplate the various ways that U.S. corporations helped support, and were supported by, a ruthless autocrat who ruled with the barrel of a gun.

U.S. Drug Imperialism

June 12, 1998

"We don't work for" consumers in Argentina or Africa, and we "don't care" about public health issues there.

That was how the deputy assistant U.S. Trade Representative for intellectual property responded almost two years ago to a suggestion that the U.S. Trade Representative (USTR) should approach other countries' pharmaceutical patent policies as a public health issue rather than as a trade issue.

This cruel and callous comment remains official U.S. policy, which subordinates the health interests of people all over the globe to the narrow demands of U.S. pharmaceutical companies.

Last month, Clinton administration officials went into diplomatic overdrive to subvert an effort at the World Health Organization (WHO) to establish the common-sense principle that people should matter more than profits when it comes to access to essential drugs.

WHO's governing body, the World Health Assembly, had before it a proposal to urge countries to "ensure that public-health interests rather than commercial interests have 'primacy' in pharmaceutical and health policies."

With most of the world ready to adopt this principle, the United States balked. Acting at the behest of the Pharmaceutical Research and Manufacturers Association (PhRMA), it suggested instead that "public health and commercial interests [be] handled in a compatible manner"—a banal and effectively meaningless notion.

When the world moved toward a compromise that would have preserved the critical principle that public health concerns should take priority over mercantile interests, the U.S. representatives successfully engaged in underhanded parliamentary maneuvers to have the whole issue deferred indefinitely.

The World Health Assembly conflict is the latest episode in the U.S. government's reprobate crusade to force other countries to adopt straitjacketing intellectual property rules for the benefit of Bristol Myers Squib, Eli Lilly, Merck, Johnson & Johnson and the other drug kingpins.

Strict patent rules provide extended legalized monopolies for drug companies. Drug companies say they need long monopoly periods to recoup their research and development costs. But no one genuinely disputes that monopolies raise costs to consumers and that generic competition lowers prices.

Many developing countries have pursued flexible policies designed to satisfy consumer needs for affordable drugs and to foster the creation of domestic manufacturers. So too did virtually every industrialized country at some point in their development—many European countries only began recognizing drug patents in the 1970s.

Among the diverse pro-health patent policies which countries have maintained in recent years: compulsory licensing, which requires patent holders to license their products (typically at a profit) to competitors; shorter patent terms than the 20 years now required in international trade agreements; respect for patents on processes, but not products (meaning competitors can imitate a product if they can figure out a different way to make it); and parallel imports—allowing distributors to buy a patented product in one country and sell it in another, to prevent patent holders from charging extra-high prices in some countries.

Countries with less strict pharmaceutical patent policies, which until recently included Canada as well as Argentina, Brazil and India, tend to have better developed domestic industries and cheaper prices—often dramatically cheaper prices. India, which had virtually no domestic pharmaceutical manufacturers prior to 1970, saw a thriving industry evolve after adopting a more flexible patent policy that enabled domestic companies to compete with the multinationals.

In the last decade, however, the United States has successfully battled for the inclusion of strict intellectual property rules in international trade agreements such as NAFTA and the General Agreement on Tariffs and Trade (GATT). Often, the U.S. position has literally been drafted by PhRMA.

Those trade agreements disregard public health considerations and have forced dramatic changes in intellectual property rules the world over.

Still, PhRMA is not satisfied. And when PhRMA is not happy, USTR is not happy.

In recent years, USTR has imposed trade sanctions or held out the threat of trade sanctions against numerous countries that have adopted public health measures which are permitted under relevant trade agreements. In many cases, USTR has complained vociferously about countries maintaining public health policies similar or identical to U.S. law. Argentina, South Africa, Brazil, Cyprus, Israel and many others have all felt the sting of USTR threats or sanctions.

It is time to put an end to the U.S. drug imperialism. People's lives are at stake in the pharmaceutical policy decisions that the U.S. government insists on classifying as exclusively trade related.

The United States could begin to break with its unhealthy past by agreeing to the modest principle that, at least when it comes to drug policies, public health should count more than the commercial concerns of the pharmaceutical industry.

The IMF Corporate Welfare Machine

August 7, 1998

In a Congress eager to do the bidding of Big Business, an item atop the Chamber of Commerce's corporate welfare agenda is in serious jeopardy.

The Establishment leadership of the House of Representatives has delayed consideration of a gigantic funding request for the International Monetary Fund (IMF), fearful that it cannot muster the votes for passage. The insatiable IMF—a multilateral institution that lends money to countries when they are unable to pay foreign creditors—is asking for $18 billion from the United States, part of a $90 billion proposed expansion.

Now Big Business is growing increasingly worried that IMF funding, which it once considered a lock, may not be approved. In an effort to solidify support for IMF corporate welfare, the National Association of Manufacturers, the U.S. Chamber of Commerce and the Business Roundtable are all stepping up their lobbying efforts.

In a letter to members of Congress, the Chamber even alleged that "continued U.S. economic prosperity may hinge on Congressional backing of the IMF."

That is quite an astounding claim. The basis of the Chamber's argument is that the IMF helps foreign economies, which in turn buy from the United States. But the IMF has an abysmal record in promoting growth in countries whose economies it has supervised. In order to receive loans from the IMF, countries have to agree to the Fund's conditions, including sharp budget cuts, increased interest rates, regressive tax increases, currency devaluation and other measures which typically throw poor countries into recession.

No, Corporate America is not backing the IMF for the good of the U.S economy. When the IMF forces Third World countries to become low-wage exporters of manufactured goods, that does not help the U.S. economy. IMF policies help shift manufacturing jobs out of the United States and put downward pressure on the wages of jobs that remain in the United States.

Big Business has made IMF expansion a priority because, for them, the IMF is a multi-pronged welfare machine.

First, the IMF bails out big banks and foreign investors when they make bad loans in developing countries—investments that are understood to be risky at the time they were made, and earn more as a result.

In 1995, the IMF contributed almost $18 billion to a Clinton administration bailout of the Wall Street interests who stood to lose billions with the peso devaluation in Mexico. Last year and early this year, the Fund orchestrated a massive bailout of the big banks that made bad loans to Asian countries. About the only pain felt by the banks was the need to reschedule short-term loans. Now the IMF has done it again, bailing out foreign investors in Russia with an $11 billion package that will go straight into the pockets of foreign lenders.

Second, the IMF forces poor countries to discard economic policies and regulations that limit the power of domestic and especially foreign corporations. That makes it easier for U.S. and other multinational companies to benefit from low wages and other perks—like weak environmental regulations—of operating in much of the developing world.

And finally, the IMF is intent on expanding its powers, so that member countries remove all restrictions on the inflow and outflow of money—what the IMF calls "capital account liberalization." This will help banks and financial corporations make super-profits in troubled economies like Russia's. Such assistance would be especially perverse given the fact that, in the event of a troubled economy's collapse, the IMF provides those investors with free, de facto insurance.

Increasingly, members of Congress are coming to see the flaws in the IMF. Many Republicans in the House of Representatives have seen the flaws in the IMF bailouts—they understand that each bailout enables more imprudent behavior by Wall Street—and are opposing IMF expansion. Now, a growing number of Democrats are coming around to the view that an institution with such a horrid record does not merit a $90 billion expansion, with the United States footing the bill for $18 billion.

The challenge now is for the bipartisan group of IMF opponents to maintain their strength in the face of the Big Business lobbying blitz to come.

[As the legislative session wound to a close in 1998, the Clinton White House and congressional Republicans entered into negotiations over an "omnibus" appropriations bill to fund a wide array of government activities. Those factions of the Republican Party that opposed IMF funding yielded, and the deal cut between then-Speaker of the House Newt Gingrich, Senate Majority Leader Trent Lott and the Clinton administration included $18 billion for the IMF.]

Ending Wall Street's Reign

September 8, 1998

For nearly two decades, the world has lived under the reign of Wall Street. It is now clearer than ever that the king must be dethroned, and the people made sovereign.

There are certainly many contributing factors to the economic crises which have spread in the past year throughout Asia, moved to Russia and which now threaten much of Latin America and South Africa. But atop the list is "hot money"— foreign loans and investments which pour especially into developing countries in pursuit of high returns but pull out at the first sign of economic downturn.

In the last two decades, countries around the world have opened themselves to "hot money" under pressure from the International Monetary Fund (IMF) and in response to a near-consensus among establishment economists, Wall Street advisers, aid agencies and development analysts that openness to unregulated capital inflows and outflows is the only path to economic salvation.

The last year has shown, instead, that failing to regulate capital flows invites economic ruin. The basic problem is that, when foreign lenders and investors fear a country may have difficulty paying back loans, they flee en masse. With investors overwhelmingly seeking to exchange their rupiah or ringgit or rubles for dollars or other dependable currencies, the value of the developing country's currency plummets, throwing the country into economic crisis. For all the differences between Thailand, South Korea and Russia, they have all suffered from this phenomenon.

With developing countries across the globe facing enormous uncertainty, two developing nations stand out for having weathered the economic storms better than most: Chile and Taiwan.

Their common trait? Both impose meaningful capital controls. In Chile, foreign investors face a stiff tax if they withdraw their money less than a year after putting it in Chile. In Taiwan, a mix of government measures—including instructions to banks not to lend local currency to foreign banks and requirements that corporations report any large sums they are taking out of the country—has stabilized the New Taiwan dollar, a feat the conservative *Economist* magazine calls "an extraordinary achievement."

Now Malaysia is looking to follow suit. On September 1, Malaysian Prime Minister Mahathir Mohamed announced that the government would establish a fixed exchange rate for the local currency, the ringgit. Malaysia is requiring the repatriation of all ringgit within one month, and afterwards will not honor ringgit outside of the country as good currency. Accompanying these measures are severe limitations on Malaysians' ability to move ringgit out of the country, for investments or even in connection with personal travel.

"What is obvious is that people can no longer stay with the so-called free market system," Mahathir said in an interview with the Malaysian newspaper *The Star*. "The ringgit cannot be traded at all so that we can regain control over the exchange rate involving our ringgit." The goal, he explained, was to reduce the uncertainty caused by speculation.

"We have asked the International Monetary Fund to have some regulation on currency trading but it looks like they are not interested," Mahathir said.

Mahathir acknowledged that the currency regulations were likely to cause some transaction costs for businesses that would need permission to acquire currency for international trade, but he argued that these costs would be more than offset by the benefits of stability expected from the new regulations.

The Wall Street/IMF approach has considered these kinds of measures a retrograde throwback to the days of command economies. But with the recklessness and failures of the Wall Street unregulated globalization approach now apparent, countries are likely to become increasingly willing to reject the orthodoxy.

One particularly meritorious idea is the "Tobin Tax," named for Nobel laureate James Tobin, which would place a tax on international currency transactions as a way to discourage rapid churning in the currency markets. The Tobin Tax, the Chilean, Taiwanese and Malaysian plans and many other proposals for capital controls all deserve immediate and serious consideration around the world.

One of the unfortunate consequences of the near universality—until recent weeks—of the faith in open, unregulated financial markets is the dearth of experiments in imposing capital controls, or even academic theorizing on the matter. Surely there is no guarantee that any particular approach will work for any particular country, or for all countries.

Nonetheless, it is clear that reclaiming citizen sovereignty from Wall Street and its equivalents in Tokyo, Frankfurt, London and elsewhere will require subordinating the needs of finance to those of people, and imposing controls on the flow of money to protect national economies.

Part IV
Corporation Nation

Multinational Monitor's 10 Worst Corporations of the Year—1997

December 30, 1997

1997 was a banner year for Corporate America. Wall Street soared to record heights. Countless corporations registered unprecedented profits. "The worry is that many companies are taking on cash so fast they can't spend it effectively," *Business Week* reported earlier in the year.

Unfortunately, 1997 was also a banner year for corporate crime, pollution, corruption, union-busting and abuse of power—a fact not unrelated to the year's record profits.

To highlight underreported corporate abuses, each year *Multinational Monitor* magazine names the 10 Worst Corporations of the Year. This year's band of miscreants includes polluters, alleged instigators of coups, human rights abusers, merchants of death, sweatshop operators, criminogenic companies and crusaders for dirty air.

Among the Ten Worst corporations is Decoster Egg Farms, which owns farms in Maine, Iowa, Ohio and Minnesota. This year the Department of Labor slapped Decoster with $2 million in penalties for violations of numerous health and safety and wage and hour laws. "The conditions at this migrant farm site are as dangerous and oppressive as any sweatship we have seen," said then-Secretary of Labor Robert Reich. Labor Department officials alleged that Decoster's workers toiled for up to 15 hours a day, with no equipment to protect them from disease, even as they picked up dead chickens with bare hands. They lived with exposure to live electrical parts and inoperable smoke alarms. Often 12 people lived in one 10-foot-by-60-foot trailer. Overused septic tanks filled up, causing toilet contents to back up several inches into shower tubs.

The other corporations on the *Multinational Monitor* list are:

- Elf Aquitaine, a French oil company which instigated a coup in the Congo according to deposed President Pascal Lissouba. Elf Aquitaine, which is responsible for about two thirds of Congo's oil output, had disputed contract terms with Lissouba, and reportedly objected to his negotiating with other oil companies.

- Tyson Foods, the Arkansas-based chicken company which symbolized corporate corruption of the political process through its illegal gifts to former Secretary of Agriculture Mike Espy. Tyson pled guilty in December to paying illegal gratuities and agreed to pay $6 million in fines and court costs.

- Virginia-based Smithfield Foods, the recipient of the largest Clean Water Act fine in history for its improper operation of hog slaughtering and processing plants.

- Philip Morris, the largest U.S. cigarette company and the leading corporate advocate of the June 20 deal with state attorneys general which would give the tobacco industry effective immunity from future lawsuits.

- Occidental Petroleum, an oil multinational intent on drilling in Colombian rainforest—on land considered sacred by the U'wa people. If drilling goes forward, the U'wa say they will commit collective suicide.

- Nike, the Beaverton, Oregon-based athletic shoe and apparel company that has made both the swoosh and sweatshops famous. This year, well-documented reports of Nike contractor workers in Asia being underpaid, physically abused and exposed to hazardous work conditions were substantiated from an unlikely source: an Ernst & Young audit conducted at Nike's behest.

- Columbia/HCA, the hospital chain which cut costs, slashed staff and put profits before patients—and is now charged by federal officials with a "systematic corporate scheme" to defraud federal health programs.

- TRW, one of the coordinating companies of America Leads on Trade, the corporate lobby to ram fast-track authority for trade agreements through Congress.

- American Electric Power (AEP), a coal-burning energy company that was one the leaders of the corporate campaign against new clean air regulations. Tens of thousands of hospital visits and premature deaths are expected to be prevented each year because AEP and its allies failed in their efforts to undermine the clean air rules.

Some of the headiness over 1997's economic performance is fading as the Asian economic crisis threatens to weaken the U.S. economy and corporate profitability. But the *Multinational Monitor* 10 Worst Corporations of 1997 list highlights weak economic performance by large corporations on scores too rarely tallied—decent treatment of workers, environmental preservation, respect for human rights, delivery of affordable and quality consumer goods and services and adherence to the law.

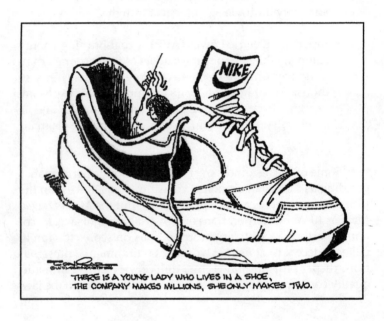

THERE IS A YOUNG LADY WHO LIVES IN A SHOE,
THE COMPANY MAKES MILLIONS, SHE ONLY MAKES TWO.

Corporate Fronts:
An Epidemic with a Cure

January 21, 1998

In late November 1997, Sandra Steingraber was on tour promoting her new book, *Living Downstream: An Ecologist Looks At Cancer and the Environment*.

In Austin, Texas, she learned of a scathing review of her book that had just been published in the prestigious *New England Journal of Medicine*.

The reviewer, identified by the *Journal* only as Dr. Jerry Berke of Ashton, Massachusetts, rips the book as the "biased work" of an environmentalist who uses "oversights and simplifications" to support her arguments.

The *Journal*'s was the first negative review of her book.

In *Living Downstream*, Steingraber puts forth a powerful argument that we are in the midst of a cancer epidemic, that toxic chemicals and pesticides are a primary cause of this epidemic, and that while we can do little about genetic causes of cancer, there is much we can do to rid ourselves of man-made carcinogens in the environment.

Steingraber soon learned that the Dr. Jerry Berke who reviewed her book was in fact director of toxicology at W.R. Grace & Co., one of the largest chemical companies in the United States.

Someone at the *New England Journal* didn't realize that Grace was a chemical company—they thought it was a hospital company.

"We should have recognized that W.R. Grace was a conflict of interest, but unfortunately the person who handled it didn't recognize that," the journal's editor in chief, Jerome P. Kassirer, told the *Boston Globe*.

As former *New Yorker* staff writer Paul Brodeur and a public health specialist, Bill Ravanesi, point out, however, it would be difficult for anyone not to recognize Grace for what it is: a company with a long track record of chemical pollution and crime, whose chemical pollution was captured in a best selling book, *A Civil Action*, soon to be a major motion picture starring John Travolta.

The same W.R. Grace that paid $8 million to settle claims brought by the families of seven Woburn, Massachusetts children and one adult who developed leukemia after drinking water that was shown to be contaminated with chemicals dumped by the company.

The same W.R. Grace that was convicted of two felony counts of lying to the federal officials about its activities in Woburn.

The W.R. Grace fiasco is the latest in a disturbing pattern, highlighted by Brodeur and Ravanesi, of the *New England Journal* ignoring corporate conflicts.

In 1996, the *Journal* ran an editorial endorsing an anti-obesity drug. The article was written by two consultants—one a consultant of the manufacturer of the drug and the other a consultant to the marketer of the drug. The *Journal* failed to alert its readers to the conflict.

In a recent editorial for the *Journal*, Stephen Safe, a researcher at Texas A&M University, argues that environmental estrogens do not cause breast cancer. Safe has received grants of up to $150,000 over the last three years—about 20 percent of his budget—from the Chemical Manufacturers Association. The Chemical Manufacturers Association represents companies that produce those estrogens.

Safe also attacks environmentalists and "chemophobia," which he defines as "the unreasonable fear of chemicals."

Safe told the *Boston Globe* that he "felt a little twinge" about the potential for a conflict of interest when writing the editorial, "but it was not much of a twinge."

"There's hardly any life scientist in the country who hasn't had funding from the industry," Safe said.

The problem at the *Journal* mirrors a broader problem— big corporate money is corrupting all aspects of society and few see the need to disclose the corrupting influence.

At least in the old days, when the Chemical Manufacturers Association or the American Petroleum Institute spoke, the public would know how to discount the message.

Now, from scientific journals to letters to the editor in mainstream newspapers, corporations are seeking to hide their identities behind corporate front groups, or corporate PR flaks that don't disclose their affiliations and list only their home addresses.

It's an epidemic with a ready cure—disclosure. Every time Stephen Safe writes an editorial for the *Journal*, he should list the money he gets from industry. Every time Jerry Berke writes a book review, he should tell us that he works for W.R. Grace. Corporate front groups should reveal their corporate sponsors.

Only with disclosure will we have a chance to rid ourselves of this epidemic of corruption. Sunlight is the best disinfectant.

The Corporate Takeover of a Consumer Group

April 1, 1998

It used to be that you could tell where big corporations were coming from because they would speak through aptly named lobbying groups.

But then, about twenty years ago, corporations wised up and realized that no citizen was going to take seriously the proclamations of the Tobacco Institute or the Business Roundtable.

So, big corporations decided to try new ways to delude the public. They set up or helped fund think tanks (American Enterprise Institute, Hudson Institute), they set up front groups (Citizens Against Lawsuit Abuse, Electric Consumers Association), and they funded public interest organizations (World Wildlife Federation, Environmental Defense Fund).

But never has corporate America been so bold as to take over an existing consumer group. Until now.

The National Consumers League, founded by labor and consumer activists at the turn of the century, calls itself "America's pioneer consumer advocacy organization."

While the League does some good work on child labor issues, it has been saturated in recent years with financial contributions from major U.S. corporations to the point where it can no longer be considered a legitimate independent consumer or public interest group.

While refusing to give specific numbers detailing how much money each corporation or industry has contributed, League officials say that 39 percent of the group's 1997 budget of $1.3 million came from corporations and industry associations.

All indications are that a far greater percentage of the League's current 1998 budget is flooding in from corporate America. And the League is planning on an unprecedented shakedown of the corporate money tree for its planned upcoming 100th anniversary bash next year.

Almost every current project, seminar, brochure, newsletter and fundraising dinner is sponsored in large part by major corporations or industry associations, with some supplemental money coming in from labor unions.

For example, an upcoming conference, Focus on Youth: The New Consumer Power, in Lake Buena Vista, Florida, May 5–8, 1998, is sponsored in large part by a coalition of major corporations that traditionally have been hostile to consumer interests, including Visa USA, the Chemical Specialties Manufacturers Association, the Chlorine Chemistry Council, Monsanto, General Motors, Burson-Marsteller, and the National Meat Association.

An April 1997 conference titled "Health Care: How Do Consumers Manage?" was sponsored by major pharmaceutical and health care companies, including Bristol-Myers, Glaxo Wellcome, Pfizer, Wyeth-Ayerst Labs, Kaiser Permanente, Merck, PacifiCare Health Systems, SmithKline Beecham, and Pharmacia & Upjohn. Big labor unions are also listed as contributors to the conference.

An Internet Fraud Watch program is being sponsored by MasterCard and NationsBank.

The annual "NCL Trumpeter Award Reception and Dinner" brings in about 40 percent of the League's annual budget. Last year, the League honored Carol Tucker Foreman, a public relations executive, and Liz Claiborne Inc., a clothing manufacturer that has been tied most recently to sweatshops in China. One of three top contributors to the dinner was Liz Claiborne. The other two were Allstate Insurance and Wyeth-Ayerst.

The next five top contributors were AT&T, Edison Electric Institute, Monsanto Company, Schering Plough, and Visa USA.

Earlier this month, the League co-sponsored with the Electric Consumers' Alliance a conference titled "Restructuring of the Electric Industry: What is the Impact?" The Alliance is a front group for the Edison Electric Institute.

The League refused to answer questions about who paid for this conference, or exactly how much money corporations are paying to sponsor the League's various conferences and programs.

The League's executive director, Linda Golodner, did not return repeated phones calls over a three week period seeking comment on this article.

But a walk through the League's downtown Washington, D.C. office reminds a visitor of the pervasive influence of Corporate America over the League's agenda.

Almost every consumer publication in the League's front office was paid for by a major corporation or industry group.

A "Consumer Guide to Choosing Your Telephone Service" was paid for by Ameritech.

A "Consumer Credit Series" of reports (Shopping for a Loan? How Much Is It Going to Cost?, Denied Credit?—The Credit Report Blues) was paid for by Fleet Finance Inc, a subsidiary of Fleet Financial Group.

A brochure titled "Making Sense of Your New Communications Choices" was paid for by GTE.

A pamphlet titled "Take Care with Over the Counter Asthma Medicine" was paid for by Syntex, a pharmaceutical company.

A newsletter, "Community Credit Link," is paid for by Visa USA.

The League refused to answer specific questions about how much money corporations are giving to support these various projects, or what percentage of the League's budget comes from non-corporate funders.

When asked why a consumer group is taking any money at all from corporations that fight consumer interests in Washington, D.C. and around the country, League spokesperson Cleo Manuel said, "I wish we didn't have to."

The More You Watch,
the Less You Know

April 17, 1998

Here's another reason not to watch television: corporate media conglomerates are getting rid of the few remaining aggressive television investigative reporters.

Last year, two such reporters, Jane Akre and Steve Wilson, were added to the list of road kill on the television superhighway when they were fired from the WTVT Fox Television affiliate in Tampa, Florida.

In a lawsuit filed against the station earlier this month, Akre and Wilson alleged that Fox executives ordered them to broadcast lies about Monsanto's controversial bovine growth hormone (BGH) now being used by many of the nation's dairy farmers.

The journalists say they were fired from the Fox-owned WTVT in Tampa after completing a four-part series on BGH in the Florida milk supply.

The series alleged, among other things, that supermarkets in Florida have been selling milk from cows injected with BGH, despite promises by those supermarkets that they would not buy milk from treated cows until the hormone gained widespread public acceptance.

BGH was approved by the Food and Drug Administration (FDA) in 1993 over the objections of independent scientists who contend that use of the hormone poses health risks to milk drinkers. Such concerns have led the European Union, Australia and New Zealand to prohibit use of BGH in cows.

Wilson says that just prior to the first scheduled air date (February 24, 1997), Monsanto's outside libel attorney sent a threatening letter to Roger Ailes, president of Fox Network News.

As a result of that letter, the series was postponed, and Wilson and Akre agreed to go back to Monsanto to give the company another chance to respond to the allegations in the story.

This drew another letter from Monsanto's lawyer. From then on, things went sour between the reporters and their bosses. Wilson says the letters were the beginning of a successful campaign by Monsanto to kill the story.

A meeting was held at the station March 5, 1997 to discuss the issue, but Wilson and Akre were not invited.

"After that, the script was reworked," Wilson says. "Changes were ordered in the script. We were essentially presented with an order to run the script in the altered fashion that Fox lawyers suddenly thought was the way to tell the story."

Wilson says that Fox first threatened to fire them when they refused to broadcast what Wilson and Akre considered to be false and misleading information.

According to Wilson, on April 16, 1997, WTVT's vice president and general manager, David Boylan, told Wilson and Akre "you will either broadcast this story the way we are telling you to broadcast it, or we will fire you in 48 hours."

Unlike many of their supine brethren within the industry, Wilson and Akre stood up to the corporate bosses. Wilson told Boylan, "If you fire us for refusing to broadcast this information that we have already documented to you is false and misleading, if you do that, we will go directly to the Federal Communications Commission (FCC) and file a complaint. You cannot knowingly broadcast news which you know to be false and misleading."

After threatening to go to the FCC, the station responded by offering about $200,000 to the reporters if they would agree to a gag order.

Wilson and Akre refused and were then assigned to rewrite the story seventy-three times over the course of the remaining nine months on their contract. At least six air dates were set and cancelled by the station. They were fired on December 2, 1997.

In the lawsuit filed against the station, Wilson and Akre allege that the station violated the state's whistleblower statute by firing them after they threatened to report wrongdoing to federal authorities.

In a two-page statement, WTVT said that it "ended the employment of the Wilson/Akre team when it became apparent that their journalistic differences could not be resolved despite the station's extraordinary efforts to complete this story."

The station also denied offering a "hush money" payment to the two reporters.

Wilson was having none of the station's explanation.

"We set out to tell Florida consumers the truth a giant chemical company and a powerful dairy lobby clearly doesn't want them to know," Wilson said. "That used to be something investigative reporters won awards for. Sadly, as we've learned the hard way, it's something you can be fired for these days whenever a news organization places more value on its bottom line than on delivering the news to its viewers honestly."

A Nation of Spectators?

June 26, 1998

The most powerful organization in our society is the corporation. Corporations have become more powerful than governments, or religious institutions, or labor unions.

So how is it possible for a group of highly educated, well-intentioned citizens to spend millions of dollars and more than 18 months studying citizenship and civic action, and yet barely touch on the issue of corporate power?

This was the question raised last week when William Bennett and Sam Nunn, co-chairs of the National Commission on Civic Renewal, appeared together at a press conference at the National Press Club in Washington, D.C. to release the Commission's final report—"A Nation of Spectators: How Civic Disengagement Weakens America and What We Can Do About It."

At the press conference, reporters were given a copy of the Commission's 67-page report, 18 working papers written by scholars from around the country, and a book edited by *Washington Post* columnist E.J. Dionne, titled *Community Works: The Revival of Civil Society in America*.

In all of this work, there is little or no mention of corporate crime and violence and its debilitating effect on civil society, of the corrupting influence of corporate money in politics or of how citizens band together in labor unions, environmental groups, and other citizen activists groups to combat the corrosive influence of corporate power on America's civic life.

In the Commission's final report, only three paragraphs deal with the issue of corporate power. Under the title "Markets and Civil Society," the authors write that while on the one hand "there can be little doubt that free markets help sustain a zone of personal liberty that bolsters the capacity of individuals to associate for civil purposes," on the other hand "there is no guarantee that the operation of market forces will prove wholly compatible with the requirements of civic health."

And what would be an example of such incompatibility? The Commission finds that "market-driven decisions of giant media corporations have diminished the quality of our public culture and have greatly complicated the task of raising children."

Of the 18 working papers, only one—written by Rutgers University Professor Benjamin Barber—deals with issues of corporate power.

And Dionne's book, like his columns in the *Washington Post*, keeps hands off the issue of corporate power.

What's going on here? It's not as if powerful institutions don't tackle issues of corporate power and its abuse. Just read the *Wall Street Journal* and the *New York Times* for your daily dose of reporting on corporate crime and violence.

But reporting on corporate power and its abuse is one thing. Doing something about it is quite another.

Imagine the Commission releasing a report documenting how citizens around the country were organizing, through labor unions, environmental groups, anti-sprawl citizen groups and the thousands of other ways citizens organize, to combat the encroachment of the corporate state into their lives.

That would be a report that could be taken seriously by citizens around the country, that could be used by citizens to help them challenge corporate power. And it would be a report that could never have been written by the Commission as constituted.

Nunn, after all, is a senior partner at the King & Spalding law firm, one of the nation's premier corporate crime white-collar defense law firms.

And Bennett, although he has a thing about rude lyrics in rap and rock songs supplied by Seagrams, is a defender of the corporate status quo. He is after all the John M. Olin Distinguished Fellow in Cultural Policy Studies at the Heritage Foundation, the nation's leading corporate think tank.

What about the other Commissioners? Elaine Chao, fellow, Heritage Foundation; John F. Cooke, executive vice president, corporate affairs, the Walt Disney Company; Peter Goldmark, chair and chief executive officer of the *International Herald Tribune*; Edwin Lupberger, chair of the board and president of the Entergy Corporation, one of the nation's largest electricity companies; Michael Novak, American Enterprise Institute, another corporate think tank.

You get the drift.

These Commissioners would never raise the current United Auto Workers strike against General Motors in Michigan, or the fight against nuclear waste disposal in New Mexico, or the nationwide citizens campaign to defeat casino gambling, as indicators of increased civic involvement.

That would too offend their keepers at the Heritage Foundation and King & Spalding.

Better to blame the citizens for inactivity than commend them for actively opposing corporate power.

A Tale of Two Mainers

August 14, 1998

Carolyn Chute and Robert Monks have little in common. Chute was born into poverty and dropped out of high school at the age of 16.

Monks was born into privilege and graduated from Harvard University and Harvard Law School.

Chute eventually returned to high school and began taking writing courses at the University of Maine. She has made a name for herself by writing books about the grinding poverty found throughout rural Maine, including the 1985 classic *The Beans of Egypt, Maine*. ("This book was involuntarily researched," she told a reporter at the time the book was published. "I have lived poverty. I didn't choose it. No one would choose humiliation, pain and rage.")

Monks, who operates an investment fund with more than $250 million under management, has written books about wealth and power, including, most recently, *The Emperor's Nightingale: Restoring the Integrity of the Corporation in the Age of Shareholder Activism* (Addison Wesley, 1998).

Both Chute and Monks are from Maine and both are concerned about the adverse effects of corporate power on society.

For a number of years now, Chute and Monks have been corresponding and conversing, relating their conflicting visions about how corporations are destroying our society and what can be done about it. Monks says that someday he hopes that their letters will be published in book form.

In short, Monks is a corporate reformer, Chute is a corporate abolitionist. It is a conflict that is bound to grow as the big foot of the corporation makes itself felt worldwide. Monks believes that the owners of the corporation can and should determine its destiny. Through his investment fund, the Washington, D.C.-based LENS Inc., Monks has flexed shareholder muscle and has cleaned house at a number of major corporations. Most recently, for example, Monks, in alliance with George Soros, campaigned against Waste Management Inc., a company with a long history of corporate wrongdoing. Monks identified Waste Management as a company with low stock value, sloppy management and misleading accounting.

Monks organized shareholders on the internet, and then forced the resignation of two CEOs. Eventually, the Monks group convinced the third CEO that the level of rot within the company was so great that the only way out was a merger with a cleaner, smaller company. Earlier this year, Waste Management merged with the smaller USA Waste.

In his book, Monks describes what he calls the four corporate dangers—unlimited life, unlimited size, unlimited power and unlimited license. Only shareholder activism, he argues, can bring about four solutions—long-term life, appropriate size, balanced power and accountability to long-term owners.

Monks believes that other efforts at controlling corporate power—including corporate chartering, investigative reporting, regulation, independent boards—are bound to fail. Only an activated shareholder movement can bring corporations into line.

Enter Chute the abolitionist. Chute is a member of The Second Maine Militia, whose goals include: banning paid political ads, limiting campaign contributions to $100 per citizen and limiting the number of newspapers or magazines that can be owned by any single person or corporation to one.

Chute is critical of the U.S. Supreme Court's 1886 decision in *Santa Clara County v. Southern Pacific Railroad* which held that a private corporation was a natural person under the U.S. Constitution. The result, she says, is that corporations "now dominate the public and private life of our society, defining the economic, cultural and political agenda for humans and all other living things."

Chute wants corporations out of politics and out of the business of influencing government.

When asked how close Monks is to Chute, he responds— "at the core, we are almost twins."

"We ultimately come down on the integrity of the individual," Monks said. "What I'm saying is that the corporate structure has enabled people to increase wealth, increase productivity, increase jobs, increase relief from pain, increase life expectancy."

Chute disagrees. "She says to me—Robert, maybe 100 million Americans own stock in corporations," Monks relates. "But that leaves 150 million who do not. Her view is that my concern with trying to reform the corporation is misplaced and that the corporation should be abolished because it is fundamentally an instrument of coercion."

Monks asked Chute to give a quote for his book, which she did. Monks put the quote at the front of the book, alongside praiseworthy quotes from corporate directors and executives. This is what she said:

"Well, I myself prefer to build a new barn and call it democracy. But if the not-so-idle-rich corporate elite wants to do a little patching and puttying on the old one in order to save it a bit longer, they might as well read Robert's book to get some helpful renovating ideas. But if faceless financiers and their tool, the corporation, aren't completely out of our lobbies, out of all campaigns, and out of our constitution soon, looks like We, the People are going to come in the middle of the night with a can of gasoline in every hand and one fat match."

When It Comes to Cancer, We're Not All in It Together

September 22, 1998

Washington, D.C. has not seen a massive citizen demonstration since the Million Man March. Now it appears set to witness a new phenomenon, the civic-corporate demonstration.

On September 25 and 26, thousands of people are expected to descend on The National Mall near the U.S. Capitol for what is being called, "The March: Coming Together to Conquer Cancer."

The March has an agenda with which few could disagree: "To make prevention, treatment and cure of cancer top research and healthcare priorities. To demand greater government investment in the public and private sectors for cancer research, treatment, education and prevention. To ensure quality cancer care for all Americans."

But the thrust of the event seems corrupted by its embrace of Corporate America.

Notably absent from The March's materials, for example, is a prevention emphasis that focuses on the need to reform the corporate purveyors of cancer. The chemical companies which dispense toxins into the workplace, the environment and our food supply get off scot-free. Even Big Tobacco—the easiest corporate target there is—escapes without a mention.

The March is affirmatively linked with a host of pharmaceutical companies and other corporations. Contributors include: Bristol-Myers Squibb, Glaxo Wellcome, Pharmacia & Upjohn, Bell Atlantic Mobile, Eli Lilly and Company, Genentech, Oncor, Ortho Biotech, Amgen, American Oncology Resources, OnCare, Schering-Plough, Northwest Airlines, the Pharmaceutical Researchers of America (PhRMA), Roche Laboratories, SmithKline Beecham, Zeneca, Abbott Laboratories, the Walt Disney Company, the Washington Post

Company, Sigal Construction and, last but not least, Morton's Restaurant Group—owner of Morton's of Chicago steakhouse!

These companies all want to be associated with the wholesome feelings associated with an event like a march against cancer. The pharmaceutical and biotech companies have a special agenda: to make sure they are viewed as cancer-fighting allies, rather than profiteers who rip off desperate cancer patients.

Consider Bristol-Myers Squibb, the world's leading maker of cancer drugs. It specializes in marketing drugs that were developed by the U.S. government and hawking them for outrageous prices.

Bristol-Myers Squibb markets Taxol, a worldwide billion-dollar-a-year seller, prescribed primarily to those with breast and ovarian cancer. Taxol was invented by the National Institutes of Health (NIH). In 1991, NIH gave Bristol-Myers Squibb the exclusive right to use NIH-funded research on Taxol, initially for no charge. Bristol-Myers Squibb played a very minimal role in conducting and funding the safety tests for Taxol. Even though the company has contributed very little to the drug's development, it has used a variety of intellectual property rules to maintain exclusive rights to sell the drug.

Taxol costs less than 40 cents per milligram to manufacture. Bristol-Myers Squibb sells Taxol in wholesale markets for more than $4.87 per milligram. The cost to consumers can be more than $8.50 per milligram.

The Washington, D.C.-based Consumer Project on Technology has documented the case of an uninsured breast cancer patient asked to pay $2,324.70 for nine thirty-milligram vials of Taxol—a dosage level often prescribed every three weeks over an eighteen month period.

"The fact that Bristol-Myers Squibb sells drugs is not a problem," says James Love, director of the Consumer Project on Technology. "The problem is that it charges top dollar and uninsured people in the United States often cannot get treatment or are financially ruined" in the process of getting treatment.

An event which bills itself as working to "ensure quality care for all Americans" should be highlighting and challenging Bristol-Myers Squibb's egregious drug-pricing policy, not relying on the company as a "presenting underwriter."

Representatives of The March were not available to comment on Bristol-Myers Squibb's or other corporations' sponsorship, or about the focus of the demonstration.

In our corporate-dominated society, public health questions can rarely be separated from corporate accountability issues.

Cancer is, in significant part, the product of unacknowledged corporate violence—addicting people to cigarettes, polluting the air, using dangerous chemicals in the workplace. And cancer care problems are intertwined with abusive practices—pharmaceutical overcharges, HMO denials of care and treatment.

The problem with The March's "we're all in this together" sentiment is that "we" are not all in this together. Corporations like DuPont and Philip Morris are a part—a big part—of the problem. A serious attempt to "conquer cancer" must take on these companies.

Pulp Non-Fiction:
The Ecologist Shredded

October 23, 1998

After 28 years of continuous publication, *The Ecologist*, England's leading environmental magazine, is having a tough time finding its audience.

Perhaps that has something to do with the subject matter of the current issue: Monsanto and genetic engineering.

Penwell, a small Cornwall-based company that has printed *The Ecologist* for the past 26 years, decided late last month to shred all 14,000 copies of the September/October 1998 special Monsanto issue.

England's stringent libel laws apply not only to publishers but to printers as well.

After the pulping of the Monsanto issue, the editors of *The Ecologist* then found another printer who printed a second run of 16,000 copies. But now, the U.K.'s two major retailers are refusing to carry the magazine on newsstands.

The Monsanto issue carries tough attacks on the St. Louis-based biotech giant, including reviews of its links to major corporate disasters involving Agent Orange, polychlorinated biphenyls (PCBs), genetically engineered bovine growth hormone (rBGH), Round-Up herbicide, and the terminator seed. (Get this: When you plant this seed, you get a plant and sterile seeds. That way, farmers can't save the seed for the next planting season—they have to go back to Monsanto and buy more seed.)

Also included in the magazine is a broadside against genetically engineered foods written by the Prince of Wales.

Monsanto says it had nothing to do with the shredding of the magazine or with the fact that big retailers are refusing to carry it. Monsanto says it did not contact the printer prior to the pulping of the issue and that it has not contacted the retailers.

Yet, it is clear that Monsanto could not have been pleased with the current issue of magazine.

Late last month, after sending the issue to the printer, Zac Goldsmith, co-editor of the magazine, received a telephone call from Penwell's.

"They were having doubts about whether or not they should release it," Goldsmith said in an interview from his office in London. "I pointed out to them that not only have we been with them for 26 years, but there had never been any conflict of any sort at all prior to this issue. I asked—'have you been approached by Monsanto?' They said 'no.' "

Reached at his office in Cornwall, Mike Ford, Penwell's commercial director, said there was an article in the issue "that might have been libelous."

When asked how he found out the article might have been libelous, Ford said, "I'm not saying."

"You are not going to get me to say anything on that," Ford said. "We were a bit worried about it and we checked it out with barristers in London. They read through it and advised us not to distribute them."

Ford said he did not know whether the lawyers Penwell's consulted had any contact with Monsanto.

Goldsmith believes that Monsanto contacted the printer before the printer decided to pulp the issue. "I'm quite sure of it, but I have to take the printer's word for it," he said. "I have no evidence to support this. If they weren't contacted by Monsanto, then that is even more scary. This company, through reputation alone, has managed to bring about what is, as far as we are concerned, de facto censorship."

Monsanto's Dan Verakis denies talking with the printer about the issue, although he knew about the issue from talking with Goldsmith two weeks before it went to the printer.

"I told Goldsmith that we would be perfectly happy to respond to questions or to offer comments about biotechnology if they were covering it," Verakis said from his office in London.

He admits that it seems strange for a printer to destroy copies of the magazine and he has no explanation for why it happened.

"Consider this," Verakis says. "We are being accused of putting pressure on a printer in an effort to stop publication of his magazine. It doesn't make a whole lot of sense for us to try to pressure a printer into not printing a particular magazine when that magazine has their issue on computer disks and can take it to any printer on earth for production."

"I can assure you, we have not put any pressure on a printer," Verakis said. "And what printer would listen to Monsanto on this when the paper has been a client for 27 some years?"

When reminded that large corporations and their lawyers often send threatening letters to even the smallest of publications in the United States and that it is tougher for smaller publications in Britain because of the more stringent libel laws there, Verakis professed ignorance.

"I didn't know that there was more leverage here," Verakis said.

When asked whether he had read the current issue of *The Ecologist*, Verakis said, "I thumbed through it quickly when I received it."

When asked whether Monsanto is contemplating legal action against *The Ecologist*, Verakis said, "at this time, no."

Neutron Jack Welch

November 30, 1998

Meet Neutron Jack Welch. He is the chief executive officer of General Electric, the world's most valuable corporation. Perhaps America's most ruthless manager, Welch puts profits above human and community concerns. Over Neutron Jack's 17 years as CEO, the company's stock value has gained 1,115 percent in value.

Enter Thomas O'Boyle. O'Boyle, a former *Wall Street Journal* reporter and current assistant managing editor at the *Pittsburgh Post-Gazette*, has written a hard-hitting expose titled *At Any Cost: Jack Welch, General Electric and the Pursuit of Profit* (Knopf, 1998), in which he raises the question—Is profit and return on investment all we should care about?

To which he answers, "Of course not." But this simple question, and obvious answer, has shaken the business media out of its complacency.

Roger Lowenstein, in reviewing the book in the *New York Times Book Review* earlier this month, makes it clear that *At Any Cost* is "fatally out of focus from the start."

And John A. Byrne, in a nasty and unfair review in *Business Week*, finds that while O'Boyle has unearthed every shred of negative news on GE from the past century, unfortunately "there isn't much muck to rake."

These critiques line up well with GE's.

O'Boyle "spent six years researching and writing a negative book and all he found was a handful of former employees who supported his biased view," GE's Bruce Bunch told us.

Actually, O'Boyle found much more than that, which is why GE's lawyers put O'Boyle through the ringer during the writing of the book.

"This was a very contentious project from the start," O'Boyle said. "GE has made many complaints during the course of the writing of this book."

O'Boyle told us that GE's lawyers "raised concerns that they had about the project."

"There was an implied threat of legal action," O'Boyle said. But he refused to make public letters he received from GE's lawyers.

When asked whether GE's lawyers contacted O'Boyle during the writing of the book and raised concerns about it, GE's Bunch at first said "that's not anything I would comment on, one way or the other."

A day later, he called back and said that GE contacted the publisher during the writing of the book because "we were concerned that the book would be libelous or biased."

"In no way did we want to do anything to prevent the book from being published," he said.

Why is GE so concerned about this book? Other books have been written about Welch, but all give him glowing reviews. This is the first to link Welch's policy's to the disastrous scandals that have struck the company in recent years.

Over 17 years as CEO, Welch eliminated hundreds of thousands of jobs, bought and sold hundreds of businesses, and shifted the company's focus from manufacturing to entertainment, O'Boyle reports.

During the same period, the company was caught in a web of scandals including defective refrigerators brought to market, industrial wastes improperly buried, excessive radiation in the workplace, fraud in military contract procurement, and the Kidder, Peabody financial disaster—all reported in detail in the book.

O'Boyle writes that to many of the people who worked at General Electric, "the connection between the severity of Welch's demands and the occurrence of repeated scandal was a clear cause and effect, as transparent as glass."

GE's public recklessness is paralleled by a private recklessness that O'Boyle details in a chapter on GE Plastics, the division where Welch started his career.

"Extravagance was a way of life at GE Plastics," O'Boyle reports. "Like Welch's Phi Sigma Kappa college fraternity, which threw the wildest parties at the University of Massachusetts, Jack's boys at Plastics were a wild fraternity."

According to O'Boyle, one attractive woman who interviewed for a job at GE Plastics in 1973 recalls being asked: "Would you f--- a customer for a million-dollar order?" The woman walked out of the interview.

"Trashing hotels was considered being one of the boys, so was playing demolition derby with rental cars," O'Boyle reports. "At the annual meeting one year in Montreal, the German sales contingent heaved a grand piano out the hotel window (fortunately, it was on the ground floor)."

When asked about the aggressive partying at GE Plastics, Bunch said "no comment."

When asked about the woman who walked out of the interview, Bunch said he would not "dignify something like that with a comment."

Welch refused to be interviewed for the book, but GE says that's because O'Boyle intended to write a negative book from the start.

For years, GE has told us they bring "good things to life." Now O'Boyle has written a book that presents the dark underside of a premiere criminal recidivist corporation.

Corporation Nation

December 7, 1998

Exxon merges with Mobil. Citicorp marries Travelers. Daimler Benz gobbles up Chrysler. BankAmerica takes over NationsBank. WorldCom eats MCI.

Corporations are getting bigger and bigger, and their influence over our lives continues to grow. America is in an era of corporate ascendancy, the likes of which we haven't seen since the Gilded Age.

Charles Derber, a professor of sociology at Boston College, believes that, contrary to the lessons our civics teacher taught us, it is undemocratic corporations, not governments, that are dominating and controlling society.

In his most recent book, *Corporation Nation* (St. Martin's Press, 1998), Derber argues that the consequence of the growing power of giant corporate multinationals is increased disparity in wealth, rampant downsizing and million dollar CEOs making billion dollar decisions with little regard for the average American.

A couple of years ago, Derber wrote *The Wilding of America* (St. Martin's Press, 1996), in which he argued that the American Dream had transmuted into a semi-criminal, semi-violent virus that is afflicting large parts of the elites of the country.

That book tried to call attention to the extent to which violent behavior could be understood as a product of over-socialization.

"The problem was not that they had been underexposed to American values, but that they could not buffer themselves from those values," Derber told us. "They had lost the ability to constrain any kind of anti-social behavior—because of obsessions with success—the American Dream."

By anti-social behavior, Derber means the epitome of Reaganism—"a kind of warping of the more healthy forms of individualism in our culture into a hyperindividualism in which people asserted their own interests without regard to its impact on others."

At the time, Derber was interviewed on a Geraldo show about paid assassins—people who killed for money.

"It was scary to be around young people who confessed to killing for relatively small amounts of money—a few thousand dollars," Derber said. "They said things like—'you have to understand, this is just a business, everybody has to make money.' I pointed out on the show that this was the language that business usually uses."

At the same time, *Newsweek* ran a cover story titled "Corporate Killers." On the cover, *Newsweek* ran the mug shots of four CEOs who had downsized in profitable periods and upped their own salaries.

"These corporate executives tended to use the same language as the paid assassins on the Geraldo show, 'I feel fine about this because I'm just doing what the market requires,' " Derber explains. "I develop an analogy between paid assassins on the street and those in the suites. In the most general sense, these corporate executives are paid hitmen who use very much the same language and rationalization. I argue that corporations are exemplifying a form of anti-social behavior which is undermining a great deal of the social fabric and civilized values that we would hope to sustain."

With the hitmen parallel fresh in his mind, Derber began writing *Corporation Nation*. In it, Derber points to the parallels between today and the age of the robber barons 100 years ago— the wave of corporate mergers, the widening gulf between rich and poor (Bill Gates' net worth—well over $50 billion—is more than that of the bottom 100 million Americans), the enormous influence of corporations over democratic institutions, both major parties bought off by big business, and a Democratic President closely aligned with big business (Grover Cleveland then, Bill Clinton today).

One big difference between then and now: back then, a real grassroots populist movement rose up to challenge corporate power, though it did not succeed in attaining its core goals.

Today, while there are many isolated movements challenging individual corporate crimes, there is no mass movement attacking the corporation as the cause of the wealth disparity, destruction of the environment and all the many other corporate driven ills afflicting society.

Derber, a professor of sociology at Boston College, says that when he asks his students, "Have you ever thought about the question of whether corporations in general have too much power," they uniformly say they have never had that question raised.

Derber says that one good way to again build a populist movement to attack corporate power is to study the language and tactics of the populists of 100 years ago. He has, and he makes clear in his book that the original conception of the corporation was one of a public—not private—entity.

We the people created the corporation to build roads and bridges and deliver the goods. If the corporation didn't do as we said, we yanked their charter.

The corporate lawyers quickly got their hands around that idea, smashed it, and replaced it with the current conception of the corporation: a private person under the law, with the rights and privileges of any other living and breathing citizen.

Thus, a quick transformation from "we decide" to "they decide."

Derber is a bit too modest to say it, so we will: perhaps the best way to rebuild a strong, vibrant and populist movement is to get this book into the hands of people who care about democracy. The corporations have us on the run, but we should pause for a moment or two, find a quiet place, and read this book.

114

The Price We Pay:
The 10 Worst Corporations of 1998

January 8, 1999

What did we learn in 1998?

Microsoft Chairman and CEO Bill Gates' net wealth—$51 billion—is greater than the combined net worth of the poorest 40 percent of Americans (106 million people).

Hundreds of hospitals are "dumping" patients who can't afford to pay.

The feds are criminally prosecuting big tobacco companies for smuggling cigarettes into Canada. (Never mind addicting young kids to smoke and thus condemning them to a certain, albeit, slow, death—can't criminally prosecute them for that.)

There's a bull market in stock fraud.

Prescription drugs may cause 100,000 deaths a year.

Two Fox-TV reporters in Florida are fired for trying to report on adverse health effects associated with genetically engineered foods.

The U.S. Department of Agriculture proposes that genetically engineered foods be labelled "organic."

Coal companies continue to cheat on air quality tests as hundreds of coal miners continue to die each year from black lung disease.

The North American Securities Administrators Association estimates that Americans lose about $1 million a hour to securities fraud.

Robert Reich says that megamergers threaten democracy. Corporate crime explodes, but the academic study of corporate crime vanishes.

Three hundred trade unionists around the world were killed in 1997 for defending their rights.

Corporate firms lobbying to cripple the Superfund law outnumber environmental groups seeking to defend it by 30 to one.

Down on Nike? Chinese political prisoners allegedly make Adidas products.

Blue Cross Blue Shield Illinois is a corporate criminal. Chemical companies are testing pesticides on human beings.

Senator Charles Grassley, R-Iowa, questions whether the Pentagon's financial controls have suffered a "complete and utter breakdown."

Environmental crimes prosecution are down sharply under Clinton/Gore. Bush/Quayle had a better record.

Bell Atlantic buys Maurice Sendak's Where the Wild Things Are illustrations to sell telephone products.

Companies that have workers die on the job continue to be met with fines. Criminal prosecutions still rare.

This is the price we pay for living in Corporate America. Wealth disparity, megamergers and the resulting consolidation of corporate power, commercialism run amok, rampant corporate crime, death without justice, pollution, cancer and an unrelenting attack on democracy.

The 1998 market run-up might make plugged-in America feel good about itself, but big business is eating out the democratic foundation of the country, and when the empty shell crumbles, what kind of chaos might we anticipate?

If you have justice on your mind, herewith for the tenth consecutive year is *Multinational Monitor*'s effort to pinpoint those responsible. It is, admittedly, a short list—the Ten Worst Corporations of 1998. But it is a representative list, and as the damage becomes more apparent, as the outrage at, and contempt for, our fearless leaders grows, surely the list, too, will grow.

The Ten Worst Corporations of 1998 are:

- Chevron, for continuing to do business with a brutal dictatorship in Nigeria and for alleged complicity in the killing of civilian protesters.

- Coca-Cola, for hooking America's kids on sugar and soda water. Today, teenage boys and girls drink twice as much soda pop as milk, whereas 20 years ago they drank nearly twice as much milk as soda.

- General Motors, for becoming an integral part of the Nazi war machine, and then years later, when documented proof emerges, denying it.

- Loral and its chief executive Bernard Schwartz, for dumping $2.2 million into Clinton/Gore and Democratic Party coffers. The Clinton administration responded by approving a human rights waiver to clear the way for technology transfers to China.

- Mobil, for supporting the Indonesian military in crushing an indigenous uprising in Aceh province and allegedly allowing the military to use company machinery to dig mass graves.

- Monsanto, for introducing genetically engineered foods into the foodstream without adequate safety testing and without labeling, thus exposing consumers to unknown risks.

- Royal Caribbean Cruise Lines, for pleading guilty to felony crimes for dumping oil in the Atlantic Ocean and then lying to the Coast Guard about it.

- Unocal, for engaging in numerous acts of pollution and law violations, to such a degree that citizens in California petitioned the state's attorney general to revoke the company's charter.

- Wal-Mart, for crushing small town America, for paying low, low wages (a huge percentage of Wal-Mart workers are eligible for food stamps), for using Asian child labor and for homogenizing the population; and last, but not least,

- Warner-Lambert, for marketing a hazardous diabetes drug, Rezulin, which has been linked to at least 33 deaths due to liver injuries.

As the millennium approaches, keep your eyes open for nasty corporate predators in your neck of the woods. Keep a list. Check it twice. Then send along your nominations for the Ten Worst Corporations of 1999.

Happy New Year.

Part V
The Big Boys Unite
Merger Mania in the 1990s

Record Levels of Corporate Mergers

January 27, 1998

With the last embers of the slash-and-burn merger craze of the 1980s still glowing, the 1990s has witnessed an even more intense consolidation frenzy. Last year saw $1 trillion in mergers among U.S. companies, almost 50 percent more than the record levels of 1996.

The new mergers, like their forebears a decade earlier, pose serious threats to society. They undermine job security, raise consumer prices, inhibit small business development, undermine the dynamism of the economy and sap the vitality of our political democracy.

Antitrust policy is the main tool available to combat excessive concentration of economic power, and the correlative centralization of political power. But the federal cops on the antitrust enforcement beat have done little more than kick back and drink coffee and eat donuts for the last decade and a half. The Clinton Justice Department and Federal Trade Commission have admittedly shown more of an interest in antitrust enforcement than their Reagan–Bush predecessors, but they have done precious little more in actually challenging mergers.

Consider the merger record of the last few years. Among others, the banking, television and telecommunication industries are undergoing a spate of mergers more substantial even than those of the previous decade.

- In banking, giants Chase Manhattan and Chemical Bank combined in 1995 to create the nation's largest bank, with more than $300 billion in assets. Multibillion-dollar mergers have become the norm in recent years. Last August, NationsBank announced the biggest bank purchase ever—the $15 billion acquisition of Barnett Banks. That record was topped in November, as First Union sought to buy up CoreStates for $17 billion.

The result: more than 70 percent of U.S. banking assets are now controlled by the 100 largest banking organizations.

The consequences of this industry concentration are well-known and not open to serious dispute. Decreased competition has led to: increased consumer banking rates (notice how your bank card and checking fees rise as the number of neighborhood banks shrinks?); widespread bank closures; the creation of "too-big-to-fail" banks that receive de facto, free insurance from the federal government; and, perhaps most disturbingly, a credit crunch for small businesses and borrowers from poor communities.

• Television broadcasting mergers have proceeded at a dazzling pace. In over-the-air television broadcasting, Westinghouse, owner of the largest radio network, recently bought CBS. Disney, a major content provider, acquired ABC. In cable, Time Warner, which already owned the fledgling Warner broadcasting network and is the nation's second largest cable operator, bought Turner, the parent company of CNN, TBS, TNT and others.

These types of mergers induce a narrowing of the media conversation at a time when new technologies could spark a cacophony of voices. This represents a dramatic blow against American democracy, at a time when it desperately needs an infusion of new energy, new voices and a new sense of the possibility of citizen empowerment.

• In the telephone industry, Bell Atlantic has taken over Nynex, Southwestern Bell and Pacific Bell merged and now WorldCom is maneuvering to acquire MCI.

These mergers threaten to stifle the competition that has driven down long-distance phone charges, and to head off competition in local phone service before it ever starts.

Slowing merger mania will require breathing life back into the core antitrust principles that guided the country from the 1914 passage of the Clayton Act until the early 1970s. A conservative law and economics movement known as the Chicago School has blinded the federal judiciary to many of the costs of mergers, which has in turn intimidated the Clinton administration from challenging mergers.

The single best hope for revitalizing antitrust law and policy may now be the Justice Department's challenge to Microsoft. Microsoft, which controls 90 percent of the market for personal computer operating systems, is trying to leverage its dominance in that market into everything from computer browsers to on-line airplane ticket sales.

Microsoft has been so ruthless in its expansion and acquisition strategies, and so disdainful of both the Justice Department and the federal judiciary, that it has generated governmental and public support for antitrust enforcement of a kind not seen in decades.

Perhaps it has required the emergence of Bill Gates, a modern-day John D. Rockefeller, to remind the nation's judges and antitrust authorities of a century's accumulated learning of the dangers of concentrated corporate power.

[1998's merger pace shattered the record established in 1997. The Federal Trade Commission reports that corporations in 1998 consummated nearly 30 percent more major mergers than the previous year. Bank and telecommunications mergers soared.]

12/2/98

123

Citicorp's Uncivil Corporate Disobedience

April 13, 1998

The Big Boys play by different rules than the rest of us.

If major corporations don't like a law, they can invest millions in campaign contributions, lobbyists and political advertisements.

If those efforts don't result in a change in the law, the corporations can just ignore it.

Case in point: the just-proposed Citicorp–Travelers Group merger. The merger is flatly prohibited by federal law that prevents banks, securities firms and insurance companies from owning each other.

For years, the financial services industry has sought to tear down the regulatory walls between banking, insurance and investment banking that are mandated by the Glass-Steagall Act and the Bank Holding Company Act. Earlier this month, the House of Representatives abandoned its latest attempt to roll back the acts.

Now, in a strange kind of corporate uncivil disobedience, banking Goliath Citicorp and megainsurer Travelers announced a merger that all parties agree the law forbids. The two financial giants intend to exploit a loophole that will let them proceed with the marriage while undergoing a two-year "review" by the Federal Reserve—a review that can be extended for up to three years. The new "Citigroup" plans to use this two-to-five year window to lobby to erase the federal prohibition on bank and insurance company mergers.

Citicorp, Travelers and other financial services companies maintain the 50-year-old separation between banking, insurance and investment banking is an anachronism. Rallying around the cry of "financial modernization," they say giant financial conglomerates would benefit consumers by providing them with "one-stop shopping" for withdrawing cash, buying insurance policies and trading in the stock market.

This is not exactly the same convenience as being able to buy milk and bread in the same supermarket, however. Even the hypothetical benefits to consumers are incidental at best.

By contrast, the new Citigroup and other giant financial houses would pose enormous risks to consumers, taxpayers and democracy.

For consumers, the risk is that more concentration in the financial services sector will result in less competition, higher charges (for everything from use of ATMs to stock trades) and diminished choice.

There is also a danger that banks will allocate credit on preferential terms to allied companies, and deny it to competitor companies. That will both raise the cost of loans to borrowers who do not have special ties to banks and distort the proper functioning of the economy.

For taxpayers, the risks are even more grave. There will be a strong tendency in down times for banks to infuse cash into affiliated investment banks and insurance companies and the companies in which they invest. (Insurance companies are major players in the stock and real estate markets.) In the best case scenario, that will make credit relatively more scarce for other borrowers. In the worst case, an insurance company's insolvency will spread to its banking partner.

Here's where taxpayers get hit: Since bank deposits are guaranteed with federal insurance—as they should be—if a bank goes bad trying to bail out an affiliated insurance company, taxpayers will foot the bill. Deposit insurance will actually encourage banks to engage in more risky behavior, because it shifts the cost of failure away from the bank and to taxpayers.

The recent South Korean financial debacle can be traced in large part to banks making bad loan after bad loan to affiliated industrial enterprises. Most analysts in the United States criticized the close relationship between the Korean banks and industrial companies—but now U.S. banks want to follow the flawed Korean model.

The most worrisome element of a Citigroup or similar financial behemoth is the threat it poses to democracy. Corporate power already dwarfs people power on Capitol Hill. When corporations reach the size of a combined Citigroup, their sheer size gives them the ability to roll over opponents.

Citicorp and Travelers have implicitly acknowledged the political control they expect to be able to exercise after their merger. In announcing a merger that is plainly prohibited under current law, they are saying, "After we merge, we're sure we can force a change in the law." The dollar and ego costs of undoing a merger are substantial. The parties would not have announced their marriage if they did not expect it to be consummated successfully.

This kind of concentrated economic power poses grave perils for a democracy already enfeebled by excessive corporate influence.

Federal and state regulators should quickly veto the merger proposal. The message to Citicorp and Travelers should be: "Follow the laws like the rest of us."

Merger Mania Hits Oil

August 25, 1998

The Big Boys are at it again.

This month's entry in the largest-merger-ever contest is British Petroleum's takeover of Amoco. The marriage creating a $100-billion-plus company would be the biggest industrial combination ever.

Conventional economic theory—the kind upon which courts tend to rely in antitrust cases—denies that one merger can set off a chain of others. But don't believe it.

Wall Street analysts, who try to live in the real world rather than textbooks, assume as a matter of course that the megamerger is likely to set off a new round of oil industry combinations, with Mobil, Chevron and Texaco among the likely targets or acquirers. The chain-reaction theory, incidentally, also explains the merger wave in telecommunications, banking and other industries.

When the merger mania hits oil, it will follow a 1980s acquisition spree (Chevron took over Gulf, BP bought Sohio, Texaco acquired Getty) and a series of more-recently formed joint ventures that have largely escaped antitrust scrutiny (Shell and Texaco have combined U.S. refining and marketing operations, Mobil and BP have joined parts of their European operations). And the oil companies have long maintained production joint ventures in Alaska and oil-rich areas around the world.

Should anyone care? Only if lost jobs, higher prices, global warming and corrupt politics matter.

The BP–Amoco merger alone is slated to cost 6,000 jobs, and future mergers will drive the total far higher. These jobs are of course touted by merger apologists as "efficiencies."

But this is not a case where labor and consumer interests are at odds. There is almost no chance these "savings" will lead to lower prices at the fuel pump.

To the contrary, the fact that consumers are now benefitting from low gas prices is widely regarded as one of the underlying reasons for the BP-Amoco nuptials. There are many reasons why gas prices are, by historical measures, now so low, but competition among oil companies is surely an important contributing factor.

In the retail markets where BP and Amoco compete directly, less competition will tend to raise prices. But even in the markets where they do not now compete face-to-face, the lost potential competition will make it easier for oil companies to raise consumer prices.

Corporate consolidation raises problems of a different sort, as well, notably the concentration of political power that flows from concentrated economic power. While no one could reasonably argue that Big Oil does not currently wield enormous political power, competition in the industry nonetheless works to limit the companies' political solidarity and clout.

BP, for example, has broken from the industry's tooth-and-nails opposition to any effort to address global warming. This sort of industry division becomes increasingly less likely as the number of competitors shrinks.

The immediate issue is whether, post-merger, BP will maintain its willingness at least to consider modest greenhouse gas reduction measures. The broader concern is that a diminishing number of competitors will lead to more lockstep, and more politically potent, industry positions on public policy questions.

Because this is the first of what, if left unchecked, will be a series of giant mergers in the oil industry, antitrust authorities at the Federal Trade Commission have a unique opportunity to nip the problem in the bud. They have not previously signed off on similar mergers, so they will not be forced to consider the merger in the shadow of a hands-off precedent.

On the other hand, if the antitrust enforcers let this merger sail through, they will have a hard time justifying action when the next oil company wedding is announced.

The Big Boys Unite

[The Federal Trade Commission approved the BP-Amoco merger in December 1998.]

One World, One Company?

December 14, 1998

How times have changed. Two decades ago, perhaps even a decade ago, Exxon and Mobil—the number one and number two U.S. oil producers—would not have dared to propose a merger.

If they had so dared, the initial public reaction would have been uproarious laughter. If the companies had persisted in their marriage plans over the din of guffaws and snickers, the laughter would have quickly turned to outrage.

Newspaper editorials would have denounced the merger. Members of Congress would have thundered about the threat to democracy and called for intensive and immediate hearings. Most importantly, the public would have risen in opposition.

There is no chance that the antitrust authorities would have approved such a merger a mere two decades ago. Now, there is a disturbingly good possibility the union will be approved.

The reason for the change has less to do with new economic analyses of the costs and benefits of mergers—though a conservative, corporate-backed campaign has managed to overturn many common-sense insights on the costs of mergers in terms of price increases and the inefficiencies of giant, bloated corporations—than with the altered conception of the political consequences of corporate conglomeration.

When the Teddy Roosevelt-era trustbusters broke up the Standard Oil monopoly, they were motivated by political as much as economic concerns. They understood that concentrated economic power translates into concentrated political power, and that concentrated political power is incompatible with democracy.

It is time for the U.S. antitrust authorities to recover that perspective—and it is increasingly important that antitrust authorities in other nations do the same.

The Big Boys Unite

A recent United Nations report highlights the importance of recognizing the political implications of mergers and acquisitions. Not only did mergers reach record levels in the United States in 1997, so did cross-border deals. In 1997, total cross-border mergers and acquisitions amounted to $342 billion, according to the United Nations Conference on Trade and Development's 1998 World Investment Report.

With the Daimler-Benz takeover of Chrysler, BP buying up Amoco and Deutschebank acquiring Banker's Trust, the 1998 figures seem likely to exceed those from 1997.

While it is the giant deals between megacorporations in the industrialized countries that get most of the attention, the hottest trend is multinationals buying up companies in developing countries. Since 1991, cross-border acquisitions of companies in developing nations have risen approximately nine times—to more than $95 billion in 1997.

(While companies are being bought up in the developing world, not many developing country companies are doing much buying. Companies based in the Third World acquired companies in other countries worth under $41 billion in 1997.)

According to the UN report, two major factors now account for the rise in the fire sale of developing country businesses: privatization, especially in Latin America and Eastern Europe, with national telephone, electricity and other enterprises coming under foreign corporate control; and the Asian economic crisis, which has given multinationals the opportunity to swoop in and buy Asian companies in financial trouble.

While it may be the case in some instances that foreign corporate takeovers will lead to more efficient company performance—for example, AT&T or other multinational telephone companies may improve customer service in some countries—in general, foreign takeovers offer none of the purported benefits of foreign investment. The acquisitions do not create new jobs, they do not generate new economic activity, they do not represent new investment—they only change the company's name.

But these takeovers do present serious problems. Where the takeovers create private monopolies or oligopolies, developing countries will face the standard problems of price-gouging and suppression of innovation.

They will also face political problems of immense proportions. The multinationals are often larger in economic terms than the developing countries in which they do business, meaning Third World governments are routinely going to have a very hard time regulating the corporate goliaths. That the company's headquarters are outside of the country, and that the corporation has no allegiance to the country in which it is operating, will make the regulatory challenge that much more difficult.

Although rich countries are more able to control foreign-owned economic powers operating in their borders, they too are likely to find foreign ownership to be a growing problem.

U.S. history makes crystal clear the imperative of paying attention to the political consequences of merger mania. But if the U.S. antitrust agencies cannot seem to remember and draw lessons from that history, perhaps it should be no surprise that their counterparts in other countries seem equally oblivious.

The Big Boys Unite

Part VI
Commercialism Run Amok

Smithsonian for Sale?

November 19, 1997

In 1991, the American Chemical Society donated $5.3 million for the creation of an exhibit at the Smithsonian Institution titled "Science in American Life." The Smithsonian curator, Arthur Mollela, made the mistake of including in the exhibit scientists such as Rachel Carson. While extolling the virtues of science and technology, Mollela also vividly portrayed its downside risks.

In response, the American Chemical Society went ballistic. According to one press report, the Society now actively discourages chemical companies from donating to the Smithsonian.

Last month, the oil companies threw a party at the Smithsonian Institution to celebrate an opening of a new exhibit titled "Oil From the Arctic: Building the Trans-Alaska Pipeline."

It is clear from the pipeline exhibit that I. Michael Heyman, the Secretary of the Smithsonian, learned the lesson of the "Science in American Life" episode—don't bite the corporate hand that feeds you.

The pipeline exhibit was "made possible" by a $300,000 grant from Alyeska Pipeline Service Co., the consortium of ARCO, British Petroleum and Exxon that built the pipeline.

The lavish opening party was also paid for by Alyeska, but Valeska Hilbig, a spokesperson for the Museum, said that the amount the company paid for the party was "proprietary information" and could not be made public.

Ruth Sexton, of the Museum's Office of Fund Development, confirmed that it was not unusual for a corporation to fund an exhibit. "Just walk around our museum and you will see exhibits sponsored by DuPont, Pepsi-Cola, the American Chemical Society," Sexton said. "But we don't just hand out lists of donors."

The new exhibit features a 21-foot section of the pipeline which is supplemented by stories from pipeline workers and Alaska natives, art photographs, maps and a 30-foot timeline.

The timeline includes a short mention of the 1989 Exxon Valdez oil spill. But there are no pictures documenting the spill or its effects.

There is no mention that in October 1991, Exxon pled guilty to environmental crimes in connection with the spill and was required to pay hundreds of millions of dollars in fines to the government and payments to those victimized by its crime.

There is no mention of the ongoing corporate harassment of Alyeska whistleblowers concerned about the safety of the pipeline.

In fact, shortly before flying to Washington, D.C. for the Smithsonian shindig, Alyeska president Bob Malone was forced to issue a public apology to Patrick Higgins, an Alyeska in-house monitor of whistleblower complaints, whose computers files were wrongfully downloaded by the company lawyers.

Alyeska funded the exhibit "in an attempt to advance its own political agenda," as Adam Kolton of the Alaska Wilderness League put it.

"They want the American people to believe they can be trusted to drill in fragile wilderness areas like the Arctic National Wildlife Refuge (ANWR)," Kolton said. "But no matter how much they spend on glitzy public relations campaigns, Alyeska cannot cover up 20 years of environmental degradation."

Rick Steiner, a professor at the University of Alaska, says that the exhibit also ignores the bigger picture—the oil from Prudhoe Bay is "simply not needed."

Outside the exhibit hall, Jeffrey Stine, Curator of Engineering and Environmental History at the Museum, was having none of the criticism. "I'm not a shill for anyone," Stine said.

"If it weren't for Alyeska's grant, this project wouldn't exist," Stine said. "But the company had no control over the exhibit."

Bob Malone, the CEO of Alyeska, told the assembled throng on opening night that the company was "thrilled to share with the American people the story of the tremendous accomplishment of building this important pipeline under such extremely difficult conditions."

In an interview afterward, Malone denied that Alyeska's funding of the exhibit was part of a public relations ploy to push for drilling in ANWR.

When asked why the exhibit downplayed the Exxon Valdez oil spill and the ongoing harassment of whistleblowers, curator Stine explained that the exhibit "is about the pipeline itself." While saying that he considered the ongoing whistleblower harassment "horrific," Stine said he "couldn't include everything."

As the Alyeska pipeline exhibit makes clear, Heyman is clearly on his way to turning the Smithsonian into an Epcot Center on the Potomac. Whether he can pull it off without being publicly chastised for selling the soul of the institution to Corporate America is another question.

Brinkley Shills for Corporate Criminal

January 7, 1998

Since 1981, a major corporate criminal has sponsored a Sunday talk show that has great influence over national public policy debates.

The host of the show and the chairman of the corporate criminal are close friends. They are neighbors at a Florida resort. They party together. The host of the show has a political philosophy that fits well with the sponsor of the show.

When the issue of crime is raised, the host keeps the focus exclusively on street crime, despite growing evidence that corporate crime and violence inflicts far more damage on society than all street crime combined. The host of the show rarely allows discussion of corporate domination of American culture, bribery, corruption or economic concentration in the agribusiness industry—all topics that would not make the corporate criminal sponsor of the show happy.

It's a very basic rule of television—don't bite the hand that feeds your show.

So perhaps it should not be surprising that after leaving the show, the host, David Brinkley, signs on with the corporate criminal, Archer Daniels Midland (ADM), to hawk its political philosophy. It is a natural progression—from unpaid mouthpiece to paid mouthpiece.

Brinkley has filmed six 60-second spots and one 30-second promo for ADM that will run on "This Week," "Meet the Press" and other public policy talk shows.

There is little outrage expressed by big-time journalists over Brinkley's move. Maureen Dowd, in the *New York Times*, was a notably exception, criticizing the corporate criminal's chairman, Dwayne Andreas for buying Brinkley's services. "It is one thing for Mr. Andreas to own Congress, which gave him a lavish tax break for ethanol, the corn-based fuel whose market ADM dominates," she writes. "But it's another to buy the services of one of the most trusted newsmen in history."

Commercialism Run Amok

Chicago Tribune Washington Bureau Chief James Warren calls the Brinkley/ADM deal "awful," but says that "most journalists in Washington are not outraged by Brinkley's move—they're envious."

Warren says that with most every journalist in Washington on the make, it's no wonder that there hasn't been an outpouring of moral indignation against the Brinkley action. He points to *Washington Post* reporter Howard Kurtz as a case in point.

Kurtz, in addition to being the *Post*'s media critic, co-hosts a media criticism show with Marvin Kalb for CNN called "Reliable Sources." This past Sunday, an ADM ad featuring Brinkley ran on Kurtz's show. In addition, Kurtz is working as a freelance reporter for ABC's "Nightline."

"How the hell can a media critic be working for two major news organizations that are on his beat?" Warren asks. As of this writing, Kurtz has yet to report the issue of Brinkley/ADM in his media criticism column.

ABC spokesperson Su-Lin Cheng said Kurtz is the correspondent for an upcoming "Nightline" piece on the internet and libel and that he is being paid by ABC for his work. She would not say how much Kurtz is being paid. "We have contracted with him to do this one piece, and we have not determined whether there will be others," Cheng said.

Kurtz did not return calls seeking comment.

ADM's hiring of Brinkley comes at a crucial moment for ADM.

In 1996, the company pled guilty to criminal price-fixing of feed additives and citric acid and was fined $100 million. The company currently faces many private civil actions seeking millions of dollars in damages for the price-fixing in a wide variety of markets. The European Community is investigating the company for anti-competitive activities. And now, Dwayne's son Michael Andreas, on leave as ADM's vice chairman, and Terrance Wilson, a retired ADM executive, face charges of criminal price-fixing.

ADM is apparently hoping that Brinkley's credibility will help repair a tattered corporate image.

"Since television began I have brought you the news... straight and true," Brinkley said in one of the commercials that ran on "This Week." "But now I will bring you information about food, the environment, agriculture..."

Paid for by a corporate criminal felon.

The Corporate Takeover
of Public Space

February 6, 1998

It wasn't always the case that the market intruded into every aspect of our lives.

Not long ago, for example, you could go to the museums at the Smithsonian Institution in Washington, D.C. without being bombarded by corporate advertisements. Not so today. Today, major Smithsonian exhibits are sponsored by big corporations. Corporate advertisements fill brochures. And credit card companies are hawking their cards inside the museums.

The sign at the credit card table inside the Air and Space Museum last month read "Free T-Shirt." But the T-shirt wasn't free—you had to sign up for the credit card before you got the T-shirt.

It used to be that you could watch public television and listen to public radio without being hit with a barrage of commercials from companies such as Archer Daniels Midland (ADM) and Pepsi.

It used to be that corporations and their markets had private commercial places, and individuals with their communities had their public places.

Today, it is difficult to find a public place that commercial culture hasn't infiltrated.

The airport? Try and find anywhere, outside of the restrooms, in a modern American airport where you can sit and read without being infected by a television or billboard commercial. The new National Airport outside of Washington, D.C. has been transformed from an airport to a shopping mall, with more than 50 upscale shops. If you get up from your chair in the waiting area to get away from the GAP television commercials on CNN, you run right into the GAP store itself. And once you get on the airplane, the television plops down in front of your face.

The public highway? Littered with billboard ads. Some estimate 500,000 billboards pollute the nation's highways. We don't know the exact figure, because the powerful billboard lobby has defeated legislation requiring official billboard counts. In the 1960s, the industry, represented by the Outdoor Advertising Association of America (OAAA), pushed through the perversely named Highway Beautification Act, to regulate the industry. OAAA supported the law because it realized that regulation was better than an outright ban on billboard advertising. The law has led to a proliferation of what has been called "litter on a stick."

Rural America? If you are fed up with the rampant commercialism that has swamped the cities and suburbs, fleeing to the country won't do you any good. Rural areas are being overrun by industrial corporations looking for compliant populations to accept their toxic pollution and waste, by prison corporations and by ugly strip mall developers and fast food outlets that have paved over suburbia and are looking to convert ever more of the natural landscape into neon America.

Public schools? Millions of public school children are force fed Channel One. In exchange for video and satellite equipment, public schools are required to make their children sit through Channel One's daily news program—including the ads. Corporations are flooding cash-strapped public schools with study guides, magazines, posters and books. Some schools even sell ad space on the public school buses.

James Howard Kunstler, author of *The Geography of Nowhere*, believes that America has evolved from a nation of coherent publicly spirited communities to a national living arrangement that "destroys civic life while imposing enormous social costs and economic burdens."

Kunstler argues that "amidst the tides of cultural sewage now overflowing our national life there is a growing recognition that we desperately need something better, more worthy of the human spirit."

The Baltimore-based comedian Bob Somerby, in his persuasive and funny one-man show, "Material World," claims that "products have taken over the planet." Somerby blames much of our unhappiness and social problems on the commercialism that has swamped every aspect of our society.

There is a time and place for everything. The place for corporations is in the market, out of the public's space. The time to begin again to enforce the separation is now.

Saving or Trashing
America's Treasures?

July 16, 1998

Can General Electric save America's treasures? Bill and Hillary Clinton seem to think so.

But Environmental Protection Agency chief Carol Browner is not so sure.

On July 14, GE Chair and Chief Executive Officer Jack Welch basked in the glow of media flashbulbs and television camera lights as he joined First Lady Hillary Rodham Clinton in announcing a $5 million contribution by his company to help preserve and restore Thomas A. Edison"s "invention factory" in West Orange, New Jersey.

The donation was made as part of Hillary Clinton's "Save America's Treasures" tour, intended to highlight and raise money to address the disrepair into which many U.S. historic sites, buildings and objects have fallen.

Though it did not manage to achieve the media bounce of Ralph Lauren's $10 million contribution to repair the "Star Spangled Banner," the flag which flew over Fort McHenry and inspired Frances Scott Key to pen the words that became the U.S. national anthem, GE did garner substantial publicity for its contribution. Notably, GE's network, NBC, did a segment on the "Today Show" on the Save America's Treasure tour and GE's generous participation.

Just days before Welch joined Hillary Clinton for their joint photo-op, EPA Administrator Carol Browner was on a more solemn mission in Albany, New York.

In an unprecedented move during her tenure at the EPA, Browner appeared before a state legislative committee. Testifying before the Environmental Conservation Committee of the New York Assembly, she condemned a GE advertising campaign which she said is endangering the public health.

A million tons of GE-dumped PCBs (polychlorinated biphenyls) now line the bottom of a 200-mile stretch of Hudson River, making it the largest Superfund site in the United States. GE is aggressively campaigning against a potential government-ordered cleanup of the area, which could cost the corporation hundreds of millions of dollars.

"GE would have the people of the Hudson River believe, and I quote, 'Living in a PCB-laden area is not dangerous,' " Browner testified. "The science tells us the opposite is true." The federal government banned PCBs in 1977 because they are believed to cause cancer and contribute to a range of other health problems.

Browner worried that the GE PR offensive would undermine health official efforts to deter people from eating fish from the river. PCB contamination has rendered the fish hazardous.

Surely no company doing so much to destroy the natural environment deserves the smiley-face association with a First Lady-led crusade to "Save America's Treasures."

The stark contrast between preserving Edison's "invention factory" and the science-out-of-control PCB trashing of the Hudson River highlights more than GE's duplicity. It sheds light on the dangers of corporate philanthropy, especially in private-public partnerships.

Commenting on Ralph Lauren's star-spangled donation, I. Michael Heyman, secretary of the Smithsonian Institution, told the *New York Times*, "We've been assured that this is a philanthropic gift and not a marketing gift."

That sentiment is comical. Virtually all corporate philanthropy—and Ralph Lauren the man is effectively indistinguishable from Ralph Lauren the company—is a marketing tool, even if it is sometimes also motivated by nobler purposes.

Typically, the public relations payback on the corporate gift far outdistances the actual amount spent on the corporate contribution.

Too often, the positive PR happy-talk drowns out voices raising concerns about serious corporate misdeeds.

The dynamic is most troubling when the company gains credit for contributing relatively small dollar amounts to quintessentially public functions—like restoring historic sites or funding schools—that simultaneously help justify systemic government underfunding in those areas.

Let the federal government restore Thomas Edison's invention factory and other historic sites. Let General Electric clean up the Hudson River.

Where the Wild Things Are

August 28, 1998

Life in Corporate America can be quite depressing.

Even the most innocent childhood moments, even our most brilliant and peaceful heroes, are being captured by the corporate machine's insatiable drive for profits and power. A major depression overcame Maurice Sendak fans when we learned last year that Max and his wild friends in his classic *Where the Wild Things Are* had been appropriated by Bell Atlantic to sell the company's telephone wares.

Why depression? Because not every image should be destined for the marketplace. Apple Computer should not be allowed to appropriate, through whatever means, legal or devious, the likenesses of Gandhi, Bob Dylan and Albert Einstein to sell hardware. There must be a limit.

Where the Wild Things Are, a wonderful childhood story, told to us, and told to our children, has now been corrupted by a very large and ugly corporation.

Where the Wild Things Are was first published in 1963 and has won a number of prestigious awards, including the 1964 Caldecott Medal for Most Distinguished Picture Book of the Year.

Remember young Max? Max was acting up. Max's mom was at wit's end, so she called him "wild thing."

Max retaliated, told his mom, "I'll eat you up." Max was sent to bed without eating anything. In his room, the forest grew, oceans tumbled by, and a boat arrived. Max got in and took off to where the wild things are. The wild things roared their terrible roars. Max rumbled with his friends and then returned home to his room. And his food was still hot. This beautifully written and illustrated story of childhood civil disobedience and adventure in the jungle is now in the hands of a corporation that charges you an arm and a leg for using the phone.

Almost a year ago, at a press conference announcing the appropriation of childhood memories, Bell Atlantic's Bruce Gordon, without apology or shame, announced that "the use of Maurice Sendak's characters by Bell Atlantic marks the first time the wild things have been used in broadside mass-media advertising, including television."

"The book is a fitting metaphor for the current state of the communications industry," said Gordon. "This campaign will remind our customers—and reassure them, too—that we are there for them through this figurative jungle of communications choices."

To borrow the title of William Bennett's new book, we have here "the end of outrage." A giant corporation, swimming in profits, decides that nothing is sacred, that commercialism has no limits and publicly boasts about its dirty deed. And the result: virtually no public condemnation.

Bell Atlantic has the unmitigated gall to rip an innocent children's story out of the minds of children, splash it onto television screens, newspapers, bus shelters, posters and two spectacularly awful billboards in Times Square and New York's Grand Central Station. And what? We stand here and take it. What's next? A computerized Bell Atlantic chip implanted inside the womb to communicate with the developing infant in utero?

A Bell Atlantic spokesperson said that Sendak rarely gives interviews and the company refused to give us Sendak's phone number. We have no clue why Sendak did what he did. But Bell Atlantic showed no restraint and it should be condemned for this sacrilege.

Disney's commercialism, its corrupt awfulness open for all to see, is one thing. Maurice Sendak is quite another. There was in his stories a purity, an innocence, an honesty that Bell Atlantic has strip-mined forever. Can we ever read again *Where the Wild Things Are* to our children without thinking of our telephone bill?

We must take care to preserve whatever private spaces we have left for non-commercial, non-market values. And we must push back against corporate greed to re-create the spaces we have lost.

Why? Because if we don't care, we end up like Pierre.

It was Maurice Sendak's Pierre who always said, "I don't care."

"Good morning darling boy," his mother told Pierre, "you are my only joy."

Pierre said, "I don't care."

"What would you like to eat?" his mother asked.

"I don't care," said Pierre.

"Some lovely cream of wheat?" his mother asked.

"I don't care."

He kept saying "I don't care" until his parents just left him there, and he was visited by the lion.

The lion asked Pierre if he would like to die. Pierre said, "I don't care."

So, the lion ate Pierre.

Moral of the story: care.

Wal-Mart and
the Strip-Mining of America

October 23, 1998

Walk into any Wal-Mart and marvel. One near us is open 24 hours. Never closes. Consumer goods as far as the eye can see. Quality product at a low price. Friendly workers greeting eager consumers at the door.

In 1997, Wal-Mart had sales of $118 billion and is on course to become, within 10 years or so, the world's largest corporation.

Wal-Mart is three times bigger than Sears, its nearest competitor, and larger than all three of its main rivals (Sears, Target and Kmart) combined.

Wal-Mart now has 3,400 stores on four continents. "Our priorities are that we want to dominate North America first, then South America, and then Asia and then Europe," Wal-Mart's President and CEO David Glass told *USA Today* business reporter Lorrie Grant recently.

And given the history of steady rise of the Bentonville, Arkansas retailer, who would doubt it?

Certainly not *USA Today*, which last week ran Grant's glowing review of Wal-Mart's worldwide operation under the headline: "An Unstoppable Marketing Force: Wal-Mart Aims for Domination of the Retail Industry—Worldwide."

But Bob Ortega, a *Wall Street Journal* reporter, reveals a different side of the Wal-Mart phenomenon in his recently released book, *In Sam We Trust: The Untold Story of Sam Walton and How Wal-Mart Is Devouring America* (Times Business, 1998).

Ortega documents how Sam Walton—perhaps the most driven corporate executive ever to walk the face of the planet—built his empire. Wal-Mart has used Asian child labor to make blouses for sale under "Made in America" signs in his stores. When he began his operation in Bentonville, Arkansas, Sam Walton hired a union-busting attorney to quash worker organizing. Outer city Wal-Marts have steamrolled inner city shopkeepers.

Ortega speaks to Kathleen Baker of Hastings, Minnesota, who was fired after talking with other workers about asking for a pay raise.

He speaks to Mike and Paula Ianuzzo, of Cottage Grove, Oregon, who blamed Wal-Mart for wiping out their photo-shop business.

In Guatemala, he interviewed Flor de Maria Salguedo, a union organizer who arranged for Ortega to talk with workers making clothes for Wal-Mart and other giant retailers.

Salguedo, whose husband was murdered during an organizing drive in Guatemala City, was herself kidnapped, beaten and raped shortly after Ortega left Guatemala City. After the attack, one of her attackers told her, "This is what you get for messing about with foreigners."

Ortega documents how communities around the country have revolted against Wal-Mart's plans to plunk down giant superstores in their communities, ripping apart the fabric of small town life.

In Oklahoma, the owner of a television and record store adversely affected and eventually closed down after a Wal-Mart moved into the area, told reporters, "Wal-Mart really craters a little town's downtown."

Shelby Robinson, a self-employed clothing designer from Fort Collins tells Ortega that she "really hates Wal-Mart." Why?

"Everything's starting to look the same, everybody buys all the same things—a lot of small-town character is being lost," Robinson says. "They dislocate communities, they hurt small businesses, they add to our sprawl and pollution because everybody drives farther, they don't pay a living wage, and visually, they're atrocious."

James Howard Kunstler, an ardent Wal-Mart foe from upstate New York, talks about what he calls the $7 hair dryer fallacy.

Kunstler argues to Ortega that "people who shop at a giant discounter to save $7 on a hair dryer don't realize that they pay a hidden price by taking that business from local merchants, because those merchants are the people who sit on school boards, sponsor little league teams and support the civic institutions that create a community."

Kunstler calls Wal-Mart "the exemplar of a form of corporate colonialism, which is to say, organizations from one place going into distant places and strip-mining them culturally and economically."

Ortega documents how communities around the country are rising up to slap down Wal-Mart's plans at expansion.

But Ortega questions whether, given the amazing popularity of Wal-Mart among consumers worldwide, anything will stop this juggernaut.

As Ortega points out, consumerism has not always held sway on this soil. Back 200 years ago, in the United States, "one did not shop for pleasure."

"The very idea of coveting goods ran counter to a broad Puritanical streak in American society, and to its proclaimed values of living simply, working hard (the famous 'work ethic'), being thrifty, and seeking salvation through faith," Ortega writes.

Ortega closes the book with a story of how Tibetans believe, depending on their past actions, people can come back to other realms besides this one.

"Among the worst of the realms is the realm of the hungry ghosts—a place reminiscent of certain neighborhoods of Dante's Inferno," he writes. "The hungry ghosts are the reincarnations of people who were covetous or greedy in this life. In the realm of the hungry ghosts, they are constantly ravenous but can never be satisfied. They despoil and devour everything around them. They consume endlessly and insatiably. It struck me immediately as a metaphor for our own mass culture."

On April 6, 1992, Sam Walton died one of the wealthiest men in America. Ortega says that he cannot presume to know where Walton went after he passed on. "But I can't help but think, at times, that his hungry ghost is still with us, in the form of Wal-Mart itself."

"Progress" Without People

December 31, 1998

MIT Professor Noam Chomsky makes the point that if you serve power, power rewards you with respectability. If you work to undermine power, whether by political analysis or moral critique, you are "reviled, imprisoned, driven into the desert."

"It's as close to a historical truism as you can find," Chomsky says.

Let's test Chomsky's theory of power and respectability with the case of David Noble.

Noble is a historian of corporate control over our lives and institutions—from technology to universities.

Forces of Production (Knopf, 1984), for example, is a detailed history of the automation of the metalworking industry. In that book, Noble shows how technology, in its design and deployment, reflects class and power relations between workers and owners.

Noble started out his academic career in 1978 at MIT. His first book, *America by Design* (Knopf, 1977), focused on the rise of the science-based industries, the electrical and chemical industry, and how universities essentially became corporate research centers for these new industries.

Noble believed that corporations should be kept off of university campuses. In the late 1970s, he wrote a series of articles for *The Nation* magazine, including two classics, "Ivory Tower Goes Plastic" and "Business Goes Back to College."

Then in the early 1980s, Noble wrote a series of articles in praise of Luddism for the now defunct journal *Democracy*. (That series has since been pulled together in book form (*Progress Without People*, Between the Lines Press, Toronto, 1995).

In addition, while at MIT, he teamed up with Ralph Nader and Al Meyerhoff and started an organization called the National Coalition for Universities in the Public Interest.

MIT, a model of education in the corporate interest, was not pleased. In 1983, MIT fired Noble.

"It was a political firing," Noble told us. "I sued MIT in 1986." After five years of litigation, Noble forced MIT to make public the documents shedding light on the firing.

"I got all of the documents and turned them over to the American Historical Association, which then reviewed them for a year and then condemned MIT for the firing," Noble said.

Next stop: Smithsonian Institution. The Smithsonian wanted Noble to be a curator for an exhibit on automated technology. Noble went to Washington for two years and produced an exhibit highly critical of technology. He includes a hammer used by the Luddites in the 1800s to smash machines in England. George Lucas donates robots R2D2 and C3PO from the first Star Wars movie. Noble calls the exhibit "Automation Madness: Boys and Their Toys," in which he documents a history of resistance to automation beginning in the 1800s. Not what the Smithsonian had in mind. They too fired Noble.

Most people think that the Smithsonian is a public institution. It started out that way, but has slowly been taken over by big corporate interests.

When Noble arrived at the Smithsonian in 1983, he figured he would have a budget to work on projects. No such luck.

"What I had to do was go out and hustle—to the National Association of Manufacturers, to the Chamber of Commerce, to various companies, to get money to put on exhibits," Noble said. "At that time, the fundraiser for the National Museum of American History was the wife of the president of the National Association of Manufacturers."

Noble then spent five years at Drexel—protected with tenure—and then headed North to the University of York at Toronto, where he is also protected by tenure.

Noble doesn't use e-mail or the Internet, but last year after *The Nation* magazine turned down an article he wrote called "Digital Diploma Mills," he published it and two subsequent pieces on the Internet <communication.ucsd.edu/dl>. The articles describe how corporations are using digital technologies to gain control over university course content.

He believes that the Internet can be a useful way to disseminate information, but not to teach students.

"You can't educate over the Internet, because education is an interpersonal process," he says.

And he laughs when asked whether the Internet will level the playing field between activists and their corporate adversaries.

"Have you noticed that—any leveling the playing field?" he asked incredulously "Wake me when it is over. It is a joke."

"The key thing about organizing is trust,"he says. "You have to have relations with people, especially if you are asking people to put themselves on the line in any way. There is no real way of establishing that over the Internet."

Whether Noble continues to get into trouble with the masters of the Internet or universities depends on whether he changes course mid-life and decides he wants some respect from the powers that be.

Looks like Chomsky is right again.

Part VII
Of Sweatshops
and Unionbusting

Fighting Back on Workers' Comp

November 12, 1997

"Competitiveness." "Improve the business climate." For the last decade, those business mantras have echoed in state capitols across the country, as Corporate America has engineered a nationwide campaign to undermine workers' compensation systems across the country.

From California to New York, Maine to Oregon, Alaska to Texas, Big Business has succeeded in pitting states against each other in a workers' compensation race to the bottom. "Cut workers' compensation costs," say leading business executives and their allied politicians, "or business—and jobs—will flee our state and move to a state where workers' compensation charges are lower."

For a decade, this ploy has worked, and states have restricted access to workers' compensation (a no-fault insurance system that provides health care and benefits for workers who are injured on the job or contract job-related diseases) and cut awards.

The corporate jig may now be up. In the most important contest of the past election cycle, voters in Ohio declared they are opting out of the race to the bottom.

By a 57-to-43 percent margin, Ohio voters on November 4 defeated state Issue 2, a referendum on legislation that would have gutted the state's workers' compensation system.

The Ohio referendum has significant national implications because Issue 2 contained so many of the workers' comp restrictions which employers and insurance companies are seeking to impose throughout the country. Among the most important:

- Excluding victims of carpal tunnel and other repetitive motion injuries—the fastest growing workplace injury—from the workers' compensation system. Ohio's Issue 2 would have required carpal tunnel victims to show that they would not have been injured without the job. That would have been very hard to prove, because people can get repetitive motion injuries from typing at home, bowling, sewing or many other routine activities, or even from natural deterioration of the body.

- Sharply restricting awards of permanent and total disability. Ohio's Issue 2 would have prevented consideration of a person's education, skills or past work experience. Here is what this would have meant in practice: Imagine that a 50-year-old illiterate man who had done hard, physical labor all his life suffered a debilitating back injury and was unable to return to his job lifting boxes. Under Issue 2, he would have been denied benefits if he could hypothetically work as a bank clerk—even though his illiteracy and work history would make it inconceivable that he ever could find such employment.

- Cutting benefit levels for those with disabling injuries who are able to return to work. The Ohio law, like many others, would have mandated hearing officers decide a worker's degree of impairment—a key variable in determining how much money injured workers are awarded—through application of the American Medical Association's permanent impairment guidelines. The AMA itself has stated that this use of the guidelines—which were written for other purposes—is "unfair, arbitrary and unreasonable."

Other changes atop the corporate wish list for workers' comp (many of which were included in the Ohio legislation) include: restricted benefits for workers who contract occupational diseases, forcing injured workers into managed care systems, placing time limits on how long injured workers can receive temporary disability, restricting injured workers' access to lawyers and underfunding rehabilitation programs.

Ohio voters took a hard look at the business agenda for workers' compensation and decisively rejected it—even though big corporations poured something approaching $10 million into the "yes" campaign (official numbers will not be available until a December disclosure deadline), at least three times as much as opponents contributed to the "no" side. By mid-October, GM, Ford, Chrysler and Honda had together donated approximately a million dollars to the campaign.

Ohio voters responded not to the barrage of TV ads paid for by the corporate donations encouraging a "yes" vote, but to a grassroots campaign led by labor unions, workers' compensation lawyers and environmental, consumer and other citizen groups.

With Ohio now in the lead, the tide may be turning on workers' compensation. The era of scapegoating injured workers and cutting benefits may be winding down, to be replaced by a new focus on alleviating the continuing tragedy of tens of thousands of annual avoidable workplace deaths and injuries.

Union-Buster Memorial Airport

February 13, 1998

Maybe they should have called it Union-Busting Memorial National Airport, instead.

That would have more appropriately highlighted one of Ronald Reagan's most notorious achievements, the decision to fire 1,800 striking air traffic controllers early in his first term. Congress's decision to name Washington's airport for Reagan dishonors working people across the country.

Want a sense of how bitter the memories are? Here's Randy Schwitz, executive vice president of the National Air Traffic Controllers Association, the successor union to the broken PATCO: "I'd rather have a hot poker in my eye than have an airport named after him [Reagan]."

The air traffic controllers' firing was about much more than the men and women who help guarantee air traffic safety. Although it wasn't the era's first large-scale firing or permanent replacement of striking workers, it certainly was the most prominent. Reagan's action sent a message to employers that they could act against striking or organizing workers with virtual impunity. And it sent a message to workers that they struck or sought to organize at their own peril. (The administration backed up those messages by appointing members to the National Labor Relations Board who had little apparent interest in enforcing the nation's labor laws.)

A series of bitter labor conflicts over the next decade and a half would drive that message home: Hormel, Continental Airlines, Eastern Airlines, Caterpillar, A.E. Staley and many others. Occasionally unions were able to resist successfully with aggressive and innovative tactics, public outreach and unflinching solidarity—as at Pittston Coal and more recently UPS—but these labor victories have been the exception.

Big business has capitalized on the new political and cultural climate which Reagan helped create—as well as enhanced power from increased capital mobility, foreign competition, downsizing and rapid technological change—to wage full-scale class warfare against working people. Employers use threats of plant relocations to bust unions; they rely on weak or non-existent unions to permit downsizing; they capitalize on technological change to speed restructuring and to shift production abroad. Many workers are so intimidated that they fear unionizing or even asking for a raise.

Here is how bad things are: The most comprehensive study done on plant-closing threats in union organizing drives found that employers threaten to close the plant in more than half of all union-organizing drives.

The study's author, Kate Bronfenbrenner, director of labor education research at Cornell's School of Industrial and Labor Relations, found that, during unionizing drives, employers regularly refer to NAFTA and Mexican maquiladoras to prove how easy it would be for them to move operations. She reports that one company in Michigan even parked flat-bed trucks loaded with shrink-wrapped production equipment—accompanied by signs reading "Mexico Transfer Job"—in front of the plant for the duration of a union organizing drive.

Plant-closing threats are regularly accompanied by a host of other ruthless (and often illegal) anti-union measures. In union organizing drives from 1993 to 1995, Bronfenbrenner found that more than a third of employers discharged workers for union activity, 38 percent gave bribes or special favors to those who opposed the union and 14 percent used electronic surveillance of union activists.

Sixty-four percent of employers in union election campaigns used more than five anti-union tactics, ranging from holding captive audience meetings where employer representatives lecture employees to threatening to report workers to the Immigration and Naturalization Service.

Most astoundingly, where union organizing drives are successful, employers do in fact close their plant, in whole or in part, 15 percent of the time.

All of this cannot, of course, be attributed to Ronald Reagan. But he did more than his share to help bring it about. It is the shame of the U.S. Congress that it decided to "honor" such a legacy.

Goodbye, Roberta:
The CBS–Nike Connection

February 20, 1998

CBS News reporter Roberta Baskin has a problem—she's not getting along with her boss.

In October 1996, Baskin broke the story of Nike's labor practices in Vietnam on the CBS investigative program "48 Hours." Baskin traveled to Vietnam, talked with young women who make Nike shoes and heard tales of physical abuse, illegally low wages and long working hours.

Now, Nike is sponsoring CBS Sports' coverage of the Winter Olympics from Nagano.

Earlier this month, CBS News reporters covering the Olympics appeared on screen wearing the CBS logo on the left side of their parkas, with the world-famous Nike logo on the right.

Baskin hit the roof and on February 6, 1998 sent out a two-paged, single-spaced memo to executives throughout the CBS News hierarchy.

"As far as I could remember, in my 20 years in television journalism, it was the first time a network news organization had allowed its correspondents to double as billboards," Baskin wrote.

Baskin alleged that her boss, CBS News President Andrew Heyward, vetoed last July's scheduled rebroadcast and update of her "Nike in Vietnam" investigation.

"I urged '48 Hours' executive producer Susan Zirinsky to change Andrew's mind," Baskin wrote. "Zirinsky told me she overheard new Vice President Jonathan King talking with Andrew Heyward, discussing a letter Nike had sent to the head of CBS Sales, expressing concern over the relationship between Nike and CBS at the Winter Games. I assumed it meant Nike probably was going to be a prime sponsor of CBS's Olympic coverage at a cost of millions of dollars and that Nike's concerns had to do with my report."

Baskin said that over the past year, she has suggested follow-up reports on Nike's labor practices when news warranted, but was told no.

Baskin said that she also wanted to respond to a *Wall Street Journal* op-ed attacking her reporting on the issue, but she was told she couldn't.

"Last night, when I saw CBS correspondents adorned with the Nike 'swoosh,' it became clear to me why Heyward had spiked all follow-up reports on my Nike investigation and blocked my reply to the criticisms printed in the *Wall Street Journal*," she wrote.

In a two-page "Dear Roberta" letter, Heyward professed that he was "shocked" and "amazed" at Baskin's "intemperate message."

"Your circulation of allegations of this kind to virtually the entire senior staff of CBS News without first having discussed them with me is not only a shocking breach of professional etiquette, but entirely unacceptable," Heyward wrote.

Heyward said he is "instructing all CBS News correspondents in Japan to ensure that the Nike logo is not visible when they appear on the air."

Heyward said that he nixed Baskin's reply to the *Wall Street Journal* op-ed piece because "I felt your proposed letter assumed a tone of advocacy that was journalistically inappropriate."

He said that the decision not to rerun Baskin's original Nike piece "had absolutely nothing to do with Nike's relationship with CBS."

Heyward denied spiking other news stories on Nike.

"The simple fact is this, Roberta," Heyward lectured. "There is no connection whatsoever—NONE—between Nike's sponsorship of the Olympic Games or any other CBS program it might sponsor and CBS News coverage of the Nike story."

Heyward said that Baskin's sending of the memo was "reckless and irresponsible."

But Heyward's huffing and puffing does not change the simple fact that CBS employees are still acting as Nike billboards. For while CBS News reporters might no longer be allowed to wear the Nike "swoosh," CBS Sports said its reporters will continue to wear the "swoosh" on their parkas.

"Yes, there is a deal," Dana McClintock, a CBS Sports spokesperson said from Nagano. "We can't disclose the terms of the contract, but Nike is paying CBS and we're wearing the logo."

McClintock said that sports reporters promoting a sponsor's product "have become part of television sports."

"During the last winter Olympics, reporters wore the logo of NorthFace, and NBC reporters have worn the logo of ProPlayer," McClintock said.

And that is part of the deal, isn't it? That's what commercial television is about—bowing down to the almighty corporation.

People like CBS reporter Roberta Baskin, who have the gall to question the practices of Nike and other global corporations will be shown the door. Goodbye, Roberta.

[According to a report in *The Nation* magazine, Roberta Baskin signed a new contract with CBS in November 1998 that amounted to a "serious demotion." Prior to challenging her bosses over the Nike deal, Baskin had a staff of four and produced segments for "48 Hours"and "The CBS Evening News with Dan Rather." Under the new contract, she has no permanent staff and produces segments for the lowly rated "CBS Morning News."]

Michael Eisner vs. Vietnamese Laborers

March 24, 1998

If greed is good, as Michael Douglas infamously stated in the movie *Wall Street*, then Disney CEO Michael Eisner must be a saint.

Last year, the Disney executive received compensation of more than $575 million. On top of his $750,000 salary, Eisner claimed a $9.9 million bonus and cashed in on $565 million in stock options.

This is not the first mega-pay haul for Eisner. From 1991 to 1995, he took in $235 million. A decade ago, in 1988, he collected more than $40 million—a compensation package which led to shrieks of outrage.

In Eisner's defense, it can be said that giant salary grabs are increasingly the norm among big company CEOs. Among the heads of the largest U.S. corporations, CEO average compensation is $5.8 million. CEO pay rose 54 percent from 1995 to 1996 (final 1997 figures are not yet in) and have risen almost 500 percent since 1980.

Skyrocketing CEO pay does not represent a massive expansion of the economic pie from which all corporate stakeholders are benefiting. While executive pay increases partly reflect rising returns to shareholders, workers have received almost none of the benefits showered on those at the top.

Average hourly earnings for working people have actually dropped since 1980, from $12.70 (in 1996 dollars) in 1980 to $11.81 in 1996. The ratio of big company CEO pay to factory workers' wages has ballooned from 44-to-1 in 1965 to more than 200-to-1 today.

There is no sharing of the economic pie here.

Rising executive compensation and flat or declining wages for workers both reflect a single reality: the diminished power of organized labor.

If enough CEOs start taking home Eisner-like wages, then public outrage may work to curb executive compensation. But it is hard to imagine a concerted effort to rectify the imbalance in executive and worker pay in the absence of a resurgent labor movement. There are no signs of self-restraint or enlightened generosity among the employer class.

As severe as the wage disparity is between U.S. executives and U.S. workers, however, the differential between the executives and Third World workers at whose expense they increasingly profit is staggering.

Disney, to its everlasting shame, has in recent years outsourced production of Disney clothing and toys to sweatshops in Haiti, Burma, Vietnam, China and elsewhere.

Last year, the Asia Monitor Resource Center, a labor monitoring organization based in Hong Kong, reported on the operations of Keyhinge Toys, a factory based in Da Nang City, Vietnam that makes giveaway toys based on characters in Disney films which are distributed with McDonald's Happy Meals. According to the Asia Monitor Resource Center, the approximately 1,000 workers in the Keyhinge factory in Vietnam earn six to eight cents an hour, far below the subsistence wage estimated at 32 cents an hour. The workers—90 percent of them young women 17-to-20-years-old—are required to work mandatory overtime, with 9-to-10 hour shifts required seven days a week. In February 1997, a combination of exposure to toxic solvents, poor ventilation and exhaustion caused 200 workers to fall ill, and 25 to collapse.

On an annual basis, the workers at Keyhinge are making approximately $250 a year.

Less than one-fifth of Michael Eisner's pay—$100 million—would be enough to quintuple the wages of each of the 1,000 Keyhinge workers—giving them a still inadequate, but at least living wage—and to pay them for 100 years! That would leave Eisner with $465 million for 1997 alone.

To call this kind of disparity "Dickensian" is to understate the nature of the problem dramatically. Globalization has wrought unprecedented and unconscionable gaps in income and wealth.

The system is out of whack, and it is going to take more than a little tinkering to set it right.

Sweatshop Deal:
Factories Free to Let the Army in?

November 16, 1998

Isn't a factory that pays less than a living wage a sweatshop? Not according to the recently announced White House sweatshop agreement.

Two years ago, following revelations that clothes in the Kathie Lee Gifford line were manufactured in sweatshops, the Clinton White House established an "Apparel Industry Partnership." The idea was to bring together clothing and related industry manufacturers, labor unions and public interest groups to work out a consensus approach to addressing the sweatshop issue.

Industry was not eager to come to the bargaining table. Years of agitation by a small group of activists had generated a mushrooming public outrage at sweatshop practices.

The anti-sweatshop campaign pierced the veil of deception by which manufacturers and retailers denied responsibility for the conditions in which their products are made. As manufacturers moved production overseas, most employed contractors to do their actual production. At first, the manufacturers and retailers denied any responsibility for the way their contractors treated workers. Then, they adopted codes of conduct, and claimed they were doing what they could to hold contractors to a higher standard.

But the anti-sweatshop campaigners cut through the obfuscations: Nike, Liz Claiborne, Disney, J.C. Penney, Wal-Mart and other manufacturers and retailers are responsible for the way the workers who make the products the companies sell are treated, the activists asserted. And, the campaigners insisted, aspirational codes of conduct are not good enough: workers must be guaranteed a living wage, the right to organize, safe working conditions and other basic rights.

171

With activists and the media carefully documenting the actual conditions in which the contractor workers toil, the criticisms began to sting clothing and shoe makers. Consumers do not want to buy shoes made with child labor, shirts sewn in hot and dusty conditions, sweaters knitted by workers working 70 or more hours a week or pants manufactured by laborers earning less than a living wage—especially while U.S. executives at the firms indirectly employing the workers routinely pull in seven-figure salaries.

Grudgingly, the companies agreed to bargain over the sweatshop issue—for the purposes of protecting corporate reputations and preventing a backlash against free trade, notes Trim Bissell, of the Campaign for Labor Rights.

Two years later, the companies and some human rights groups have reached an agreement—but the two unions and one public interest group that were part of the Apparel Industry Partnership have balked at the deal.

The Apparel Industry Partnership proposal would create a new organization, the Fair Labor Association (FLA), with a board equally divided between business representatives on the one hand, and labor and public interest organizations on the other. The FLA would accredit independent monitors to determine if companies are meeting a Workplace Code of Conduct. The Code prohibits forced or child labor (by children under 14 or 15), bans harassment or abuse, recognizes employees' right to organize and sets a maximum 60-hour work week. Employers that are certified as in compliance with the Code of Conduct would be able to tout the FLA's seal of approval.

Legitimate labor rights groups agreed to the FLA proposal, but it was denounced by many others.

"The Fair Labor Association neither represents labor nor is fair," says Medea Benjamin, co-director of the human rights group Global Exchange. "This agreement will allow corporations to continue paying poverty wages, violate labor rights and hide their factories overseas."

The deal does not recognize the right of workers to a living wage, the most basic of demands.

Assuming that company recognition of employees' right to organize has any meaning whatsoever, it is very unclear what effect it would have in countries where governments do not respect workers' organizing rights (say China, to take one not-so-incidental example). The Apparel Industry Partnership agreement says that in these countries, companies and their contractors "shall not affirmatively seek the assistance of state authorities to prevent workers from exercising these rights."

As UNITE, the clothing and textile union, explained in a searing commentary, "This presumably means you can let the army in the door, but you can't call them."

Critics have also raised serious issues about the basic workings of the plan. The independent monitoring scheme effectively lets companies pick which of their factories will be monitored, for example.

Serious questions deserve to be raised about any approach to global production questions which accepts the principle that corporations have a right to move factories wherever they wish. And it is clear why Big Business's concern with the bottom line would prevent them from conceding on this principle.

But far less is at stake in dollars-and-cents terms when it comes to paying a living wage in poor countries—whether Nike workers make five dollars a day instead of two, say, will have little discernible effect on the company's bottom line.

Could it be that the real corporate fear in genuinely recognizing the right of Third World workers to earn a living wage and organize without intimidation is that workers in the United States might demand such rights, too?

NAFTAshock

December 24, 1998

It has been a five-year party for multinational corporations, which will celebrate the fifth anniversary of the implementation of the North American Free Trade Agreement (NAFTA) on January 1, 1999.

Unfortunately, the corporate CEOs have been dancing on the heads of the rest of us.

While NAFTA has made its contribution to soaring corporate profitability over the last half decade, it has degraded jobs, living standards, the environment and democracy in both the United States and Mexico, as well as in Canada.

When the United States debated NAFTA—imagine, a time when the national debate concerned matters central to the evolution of the political economy!—labor unions, consumer groups, environmentalists and others issued a straightforward critique. Under NAFTA, they said, corporations would move South in order to exploit Mexico's cheap labor and weak environmental protections. And even corporations that remained in the United States, they contended, would use the threat of relocation to leverage bargaining power over workers, communities and governments.

NAFTA proponents told a different story. They said that increased exports to Mexico would create hundreds of thousands of new, good-paying jobs in the United States, while increased foreign investment in Mexico would raise Mexican living conditions. Pessimists' alarmism was misplaced, they said, noting that the trade deal even had attached "side agreements" specifically designed to protect labor rights and the environment.

More than enough time has now passed to assess who was right. Unfortunately, the critics' fears have come to pass, while the proponents' promises have proven illusory.

A new, extremely well documented report card from Public Citizen's Global Trade Watch gives NAFTA a failing grade in U.S. job creation and job quality, agriculture, the environment, public health, wage levels in the United States and Mexico, economic development and living standards in Mexico, sovereignty and democratic governance and highway safety.

Consider the central issue of jobs and wages.

A single narrow U.S. government program that tracks trade-related job loss has now certified the loss of more than 200,000 specific U.S. jobs due to NAFTA. Proponents are completely unable to point to offsetting jobs created as a result of NAFTA. Indeed, the Public Citizen report card notes, "several years ago the U.S. Commerce Department canceled its program of bi-annual surveys of U.S. companies to document NAFTA job creation because the data was so embarrassing—fewer than 1,500 specific jobs could be documented."

The actual figure for job loss is almost certainly far worse than the government figures suggest. Under NAFTA, the U.S. $1.7 billion trade surplus with Mexico has flipped into a massive trade deficit, estimated at $14.7 billion for 1998.

It is of course the case that the unemployment rate in the United States is now quite low, at least by recent historical standards. But under NAFTA, good-paying manufacturing jobs have been rapidly replaced by low-wage service jobs—cashiers, janitors, retail clerks.

The remaining manufacturing jobs are under severe pressure. While factory jobs in the United States pay, on average, more than $18 an hour, maquiladora workers in high-tech foreign plants in Mexico earn about a buck and a half an hour.

Employers have made explicit use of the threat to move to Mexico to beat back union organizing efforts, as well as to deny demands for wage increases. Cornell researcher Kate Bronfenbrenner has documented a tripling of employer plant-closing threats during union organizing drives since NAFTA's adoption.

Meanwhile, NAFTA has simultaneously failed to deliver the touted benefits for Mexico. In a kind of mutant industrialization, NAFTA has turned huge swaths of the country into a processor of goods for export to the United States. The nationwide export processing zone model has proved an abject failure. There are few linkages between the export factories and the rest of the economy. Small Mexican business has collapsed. Workers' productivity is up 36 percent since NAFTA went into effect, but Mexican wages fell 29 percent between 1993 and 1997.

Though the story is less stark in other areas, the Public Citizen report card makes clear that NAFTA deserves an "F" in every subject.

A failure for citizens, a party for Big Business. It is time to end the NAFTA nightmare. NAFTA—and the model in which corporations are able to drag down labor, environmental and consumer standards by pitting countries against each other in a race to the bottom—must be scrapped.

Part VIII
Do I Have to Arrest You?
Corporations and the Law

Judge to GM:
Do I Have to Arrest You?

March 6, 1998

Sometimes it takes a threat of jail time for corporate lawyers to abide by the law.

Attorneys for General Motors, threatened with imprisonment for contempt, last month turned over internal documents that are likely to undermine the giant automaker's defense in product liability cases around the country.

In Fort Lauderdale, Florida, Broward County Judge Arthur Franza ordered GM to turn over the documents in a lawsuit brought by the parents of 13-year-old Shane McGee. Shane was killed in 1991 when the fuel tank in the 1983 Oldsmobile Cutlass station wagon he was riding in burst into flames after being struck in the rear by another vehicle.

GM fought to keep the documents secret, but at a showdown hearing on February 5, Judge Franza threatened "very severe sanctions" if GM did not obey his order.

Pursuant to a subpoena, GM's in-house attorney Glenn Jackson appeared before Judge Franza on that day, but did not bring with him the documents that Franza had ordered him to bring to court. Jackson, GM's case manager for the McGee lawsuit, told the Judge that GM would not give him the documents to bring to trial.

"Do I have to arrest you, and book you, and put you on bond and release you?" Judge Franza asked Jackson. "I am warning you all and your client to produce these documents by Monday. Let me tell you, if you don't, there is going to be some very severe sanctions, and I mean very severe. I don't think General Motors is big enough to thumb its nose at the court. I don't think they are big enough to obstruct justice or to conceal evidence."

On February 9, GM finally produced the documents that it had sought for years to keep secret. Judge Franza conducted an evidentiary review, and ordered a number of them admitted into evidence.

The legal skirmishing centers around a dispute between two former General Motors engineers, Edward Ivey and Ronald Elwell.

On June 29, 1973, Ivey, then an engineer at Oldsmobile, prepared a two-page report and calculated that fatalities related to fuel-fed fires were costing GM $2.40 per automobile.

Ivey multiplied 500 fatalities times an estimated $200,000 per fatality ($100 million) and divided that by 41 million automobiles. "This cost will be with us until a way of preventing all crash-related fuel-fed fires is developed," Ivey concluded.

The Ivey report, as it is known, has been used by plaintiffs attorneys against GM in fuel-fed fire cases for almost 10 years now. But there has been an ongoing dispute between Ivey and Elwell about why Ivey prepared the report and what he meant by it.

Elwell, a retired GM engineer and whistleblower, testified in the McGee case that in 1981, the Ivey report appeared on his desk at General Motors in a plain brown envelope. Elwell said that the Ivey report had on it a cover sheet which showed it was distributed to GM management.

Elwell testified that after reading the report, he met Ivey in an Oldsmobile garage and Ivey told him he prepared the report at the request of GM management "because General Motors wanted to know how much they could spend on fuel systems."

Ivey says he had never met with Elwell and that he did not know why he prepared the report or who asked him to prepare it. "I don't remember anyone asking me to write it and I don't believe anyone did," Ivey said.

In May 1997, McGee's attorney sought from GM any documents relating to the Ivey report. GM said that no such documents existed.

But after the February 5 showdown, GM produced the documents, one of which is a legal summary of an interview conducted with Ivey on November 3, 1981.

In that document, GM attorneys conclude that "Ivey is not an individual whom we would ever, in any conceivable situation, want to be identified" to plaintiffs attorneys in fuel-fed fire cases "and the documents he generated are undoubtedly some of the potentially most harmful and most damaging were they ever to be produced."

This document also appears to contradict Ivey's claim that he doesn't know why he prepared the report. In the document prepared by GM attorneys, Ivey said he wrote the report "for Oldsmobile management" and engineers to "assist them in 'trying to figure out how much Olds could spend on fuel systems.' "

GM doesn't want anyone to think it was a cheapskate, unwilling to spend more than $2.40 per car to fix the problem. In a statement last week, GM said that "a dollar value cannot be placed on human life" and that "any suggestion that GM does not care about occupant and product safety is reprehensible and couldn't be further from the truth."

Whatever you say, big boy.

The Corporate Seminar for Judges

March 18, 1998

In *A Civil Action*, the bestselling non-fiction book about a toxic tort case, Harvard Law School Professor Charles Nesson plays a pivotal role.

Jan Schlictmann, the plaintiffs' lawyer and star of the book, persuades Nesson to join the legal team advising the residents of Woburn, Massachusetts in their lawsuit against chemical companies for polluting the town's drinking water supplies.

The author of the book, Jonathan Harr, quotes Nesson as saying: "The only lesson that corporations understand is money. Sales, income, earnings, profit, the bottom line. That is their blood."

Because the book has been on the best-seller list for more than two years now, Nesson has gained a bit of a reputation as a crusading anti-corporate lawyer.

But don't be misled. Nesson's current work is being funded by America's giant corporations.

As part of the Berkman Center, Nesson has set up something called The Daubert Project. The Daubert Project holds seminars around the country for judges about the implications of the Supreme Court's 1993 decision in *Daubert v. Merrell Dow Pharmaceuticals, Inc.*

Nesson, along with fellow Harvard Law Professor Charles Fried, submitted a friend-of-the-court brief on behalf of Merrell Dow's position in the case.

In *Daubert*, the plaintiffs sought to introduce evidence that birth defects had been caused by a mother's ingestion of the anti-nausea drug Bendectin.

Despite the fact that the Supreme Court sided with the plaintiffs in *Daubert*, by setting up a process for judges to determine the reliability and relevancy of scientific evidence, the decision gives trial judges important powers to exclude scientific evidence and thus undermine plaintiffs' chances in toxic tort cases.

"The *Daubert* formula strikes many trial judges as a whispered invitation to unconstitutionally invade the province of the jury in weighing the evidence of causation in toxic tort cases," says Rob Hager, a Washington, D.C. plaintiffs' attorney.

Nesson's Daubert Project now is holding seminars around the country in an effort to educate judges about their role as evidentiary gatekeepers.

Eight such seminars have been held so far, including one in Jacksonville, Florida titled "The Judge's Role as Gatekeeper: Responsibilities and Powers."

More than 300 state and federal judges from Florida attended the Jacksonville seminar. Each received materials prepared by Nesson and his colleagues at Harvard. On the front orange cover of the materials are the words "Produced by The Daubert Project, Berkman Center on Law & Technology, Harvard Law School."

What the participants were not told is that the Daubert Project is funded in part by a $300,000 grant from the Civil Justice Reform Group, a "tort reform" lobby group made up of general counsel of 60 of the nation's largest corporations.

The Civil Justice Reform Group's operating committee is headed by Mike Withrow, associate general counsel at Procter & Gamble. Withrow says that Procter & Gamble has donated an additional $100,000 to the Berkman Center.

Withrow says that his group's $300,000 donation should help cover the costs of 10 state conferences in 1997 and an additional seven to nine conferences that will be held in 1998.

"All we want to do is present a balanced program," Withrow says. "We want good science."

Don't tell that to Christian Searcy.

Searcy, a West Palm Beach trial attorney who was on the panel with Nesson discussing *Daubert* at the Jacksonville seminar, says that going into the event, his impression was that "the purpose of the presentation was to have a law professor put on an objective program about evidence."

"After participating in the program, it was my impression that Professor Nesson was an advocate for the proposition of judges excluding expert testimony in products liability or scientific cases," Searcy says. "The method he conducted the program seemed to me to be slanted toward persuading people to be more restrictive in keeping scientific evidence out."

"The end effect of having someone with an agenda put on a program that purports to be academic and objective is that you mislead the audience," Searcy says. "It reminds you of the wolf in sheep's clothing."

Robert Hanson works for the Florida court system and put together the program. Hanson also was surprised to hear about The Daubert Project's funding.

"My impression was the program was being funded by Harvard," Hanson says.

Nesson says that he does not tell the judges where the money for The Daubert Project comes from. "We have just said this is a Berkman Center project," Nesson says. "We haven't gone around advertising where the money is coming from."

As for any reputation of being supportive of plaintiffs in toxic tort cases, Nesson says, "I don't think I'm on any side."

"I want credible verdicts," he says. "If verdicts are not credible, the whole system suffers. And in fact that is what was happening."

Nesson says that he would be "delighted to have continuing support" from big corporations.

The better to see you with, my dear.

Destroy the Dummy,
Destroy the Child

May 1, 1998

On October 15, 1995, Robert Sanders lost his seven-year-old daughter, Alison. Alison Sanders was riding in the front passenger seat of a three-week-old 1995 Dodge Caravan in Baltimore, Maryland. The van, traveling at 9.3 miles per hour, struck a car in front of it. The air bag deployed, killing Alison.

Robert Sanders, a business lawyer in Baltimore, was besides himself with grief. He checked himself into a psychiatric hospital for three weeks following the death of his daughter.

Now, Robert Sanders is on a campaign to fix the problem of unsafe air bags. Alison Sanders and more than 90 others, mostly children and women, have been killed by air bags over the past three years.

Sanders is the founder of Parents for Safer Air Bags, a group of parents of children killed by air bags.

Sanders says that some air bags are safer than others. For example, some air bags fire out directly at the occupant. Safer air bags shoot up along the windshield and thus pose less of a risk to the occupant. Many other safety features are also already in vehicles on the road today.

At an April press conference in Washington, D.C., Parents for Safer Air Bags called on the National Highway Traffic Safety Administration (NHTSA) to upgrade its air bag safety tests to prevent front-seat passengers from being killed or seriously injured by poorly designed air bags.

The group petitioned the agency to expand the present tests which currently use only a properly positioned dummy representing a 170-pound male in a 30-mph crash test and do not test for vehicle occupants of other sizes in other positions.

Air bags have saved hundreds of lives and are a major step forward in advancing auto safety—but they have also killed 96 people, including fifty-four children under age 11 and twenty-five women shorter than five feet, four inches.

"Ten children have been killed and six others severely injured in Chrysler minivans, yet the company deliberately chose not to test the bags in its family-style minivans with child dummies," Sanders said.

Asked why Chrysler didn't test its air bags using child dummies, Chrysler's senior vehicle safety specialist, Howard Willson, testified recently in a deposition in a defective production lawsuit that "you'd destroy the dummy so there was little purpose in testing something where you knew the result was—could be catastrophic as far as the dummy was concerned."

During his deposition, Willson said he "can't say it was a surprise" when he heard that air bags were killing children.

Sanders says he was shocked when he heard about Willson's testimony.

"Chrysler marketed its family-style minivans of the 1990s with photographs of a little leaguer sitting in the front seat of a minivan," Sanders said. "Yet we now learn from the testimony of Howard Willson that Chrysler never crash tested any of its minivans with child-sized dummies, because according to Willson, the company knew that the air bag would 'destroy' the child-sized dummy. By inference, they understood that the air bag would also destroy the child."

In states in which juries are permitted to impose punitive damages, this testimony presents a serious problem for Chrysler, which faces numerous lawsuits from parents who have lost children to Chrysler air bags.

Many manufacturers have deliberately chosen air bag designs that meet the minimum federal standard but which are dangerous for children and women at low-speed collisions.

Now, the auto companies are lobbying Congress and the Department of Transportation to go slow and not set any firm deadlines for setting a proper air bag safety standard.

In September 1996, the National Transportation Safety Board issued an "urgent" safety recommendation that NHTSA "immediately revise" the air bag performance standard to "establish performance requirements that reflect the actual accident environment."

Despite's NHTSA's announcement that it would propose an upgrade in early 1997, no such proposed rule has been issued.

While some manufacturers have incorporated widely available technology in their air bag designs that address real-world crash conditions, many have not.

According to NHTSA data, eight manufacturers—Alfa Romeo, BMW, Honda, Mercedes Benz, Nissan, Porsche, Saab and Subaru—have had no passenger-side air bag deaths or severe injuries. But other companies have installed poorly designed air bags which have resulted in deaths and severe injuries.

To honor the lives of those little ones who have been killed because corporate executives refused to do the right thing, the government must act promptly to require proper testing of these important safety devices. And those corporations responsible for the carnage must be brought to justice.

First Amendment Follies

June 5, 1998

It is time for the people to take back the First Amendment. In recent years, corporations rather than people are increasingly invoking the First Amendment to defend controversial speech. In extending Bill of Rights protections to corporations and stiffening commercial speech protections, the courts are increasingly shielding antisocial corporate behavior.

Consider ongoing efforts in the U.S. Congress to regulate Big Tobacco. Among the regulations being considered are strong advertising and marketing restrictions that would prohibit tobacco billboard advertisements, restrict tobacco print ads to black-and-white, text-only format in publications with high youth readership and ban the use of human images and cartoons in tobacco promotions.

The tobacco industry and its defenders in Congress, as well as its allies in academia, have rushed to declare all of these proposed restrictions unconstitutional.

The problem is, they may well be right, at least under recent Supreme Court rulings. Commercial speech now receives almost the same safeguards as political speech, with the government required to overcome a series of hurdles before it can limit non-fraudulent commercial speech (the speech restriction must further a government interest; it must directly advance the interest; and there must not be available less-restrictive alternatives to accomplish the same ends). And speech by corporations is treated as no different than speech by people.

Under prevailing doctrine, the government would have a very hard time regulating cigarette advertising as a public health policy to deter use of a deadly product. Instead, it must justify its restrictions on the grounds that certain kinds of advertisements appeal to children. And then it must justify advertising limitations against alternative regulatory approaches (even approaches that should be complimentary), such as efforts to limit cigarette sales to minors.

Northwestern University constitutional law scholar Martin Redish takes the argument even further. Since the speech of anti-tobacco advocates is plainly protected by the First Amendment, he says, tobacco company advertisements—designed to encourage people to smoke—deserve equal protection. And Redish's argument, not now the law, may well signal where it is heading.

This is absurd. There is no reason major public health initiatives should be held hostage to the purported "rights" of private, for-profit corporations selling and marketing a product that every year kills hundreds of thousands of people in the United States alone.

The law has gone awry in treating corporations as entitled to many of the same constitutional protections, including First Amendment guarantees, as real people.

The consequences are not limited only to preserving the advertising rights of the legal "vice" industries (tobacco, alcohol, gambling).

Corporations have invoked their speech rights to defeat desirable initiatives ranging from a Vermont program requiring labeling of milk from cows treated with BGH (bovine growth hormone, also known as BST) to a California law that would have required utilities, at no cost to the utilities, to include in their billing envelopes an invitation to join an independent consumer group. In both of these examples, courts ruled that the laws would violate corporations' right not to speak.

At the same time as they've become such strident defenders of First Amendment freedoms, corporations—with increasing frequency—are intimidating citizens from exercising their free speech rights. These corporations are charging citizen activists who speak out about alleged corporate wrongdoing with defamation, libel, slander and tortious interference with contract, and suing them for large sums of money. Most of the corporate suits fail, but they have the desired effect of tying up activists' time, and intimidating them and others from speaking out.

It is time to redirect First Amendment law. The simple solution to the problem is to deny corporations First Amendment protections. Extending constitutional protections to corporations hurts democracy by putting artificial entities with enormous resource and legal advantages (limited liability, perpetual life, inability to be jailed) on the same footing as people.

Moving the law—which turns with the speed of an ocean liner—in this direction will be a major challenge. Steady advocacy from legal scholars can nudge the law in a more democratic direction, but it will require a tidal wave of outrage from a citizenry fed up with uncontrolled corporate power to reverse the course of First Amendment jurisprudence.

Holding Gun Corporations Responsible

June 12, 1998

Last week, Philadelphia Mayor Ed Rendell met with top executives from major handgun manufacturers Smith & Wesson, Glock Inc., O.F. Mossberg, and an industry trade group, the American Shooting Sports Council.

Why? The handgun industry is concerned that the city of Philadelphia is about to file a lawsuit seeking to hold the companies liable for the gun violence that claims one human life every day in the city.

The United States leads the world in people who are killed and injured by handguns—25,000 a year dead, compared to a few hundred in every other industrialized country.

Last year, the police in the city of Philadelphia, together with a diverse group of citizen activists, came together as the Youth Violence Task Force to discuss possible solutions to the gun violence in the city.

Unlike most other cities, where handgun violence has decreased dramatically over the past couple of years, Philadelphia has seen a steady flow of bloodshed.

Philadelphia police officers teamed up with agents from the Bureau of Alcohol, Tobacco and Firearms to research the problem. They tracked all 38,000 handgun sales in the Philadelphia area over the course of a year and made a startling finding. Fully 30 percent of the handguns purchased in the Philadelphia area were purchased by someone who bought three or more in that period and averaged over five—more than any individual might conceivably need for the ostensible purpose of self-defense. Nine percent of the purchasers are buying 30 percent of the handguns in the Philadelphia area.

This was an eye-opener to task force member David Kairys, whose day job is professor of law at Temple University

Law School. Kairys concluded that gun manufacturers are feeding off the criminal element.

"The companies use our lax laws and our cultural glorification of guns and violence to deflect attention from themselves," Kairys told us. "And the city of Philadelphia is going to incur costs connected with the product, starting with a 911 call, cleaning up blood off the streets, medical costs, which in some cities are borne by the city, all the way to the support of a child who might be orphaned as a result of gun violence."

Kairys drafted a memo on how Philadelphia could hold the gun manufacturers liable for the bloodshed caused by guns. Mayor Ed Rendell, who is planning a run for governor of Pennsylvania, liked the memo and hired Kairys to draft a lawsuit against the major gun companies.

Kairys concedes that the companies cannot be held liable under current product liability law because, generally speaking, guns are not defective—they kill as advertised.

Instead, Kairys proposes suing the manufacturers for negligence, public nuisance and fraud.

The companies create a public nuisance by interfering with the public's right to health, safety and peace by funnelling handguns to criminals.

In support of this argument, Kairys cites the testimony of Robert Hass, former executive at Smith & Wesson, the nation's largest handgun manufacturer.

"The company and the industry as a whole are fully aware of the extent of the criminal misuse of firearms," Hass testified in a New York case in 1996. "The company and the industry are also aware that the black market in firearms is not simply the result of stolen guns but is due to the seepage of guns into the illicit market from multiple thousands of unsupervised federal firearms licensees. In spite of their knowledge, however, the industry's position has consistently been to take no independent action to insure responsible distribution practices."

Kairys cites the rapid-firing Intratec DC-9s, promoted by the manufacturer for its "excellent resistance to fingerprints."

He also cites advertisements from gun magazines and general circulation journals such as *Ladies Home Journal*, which advertise guns as necessary to keep everyone in the house safe.

Kairys argues that such claims are fraudulent and negligent.

"If you bring a gun into your home, it is several times more likely that someone will die by a gun," Kairys reports. "And it is five times more likely you will have a suicide, and 10 times more likely you will have a suicide if you have a teenager in your home."

Kairys began drafting a lawsuit to present to Rendell. But in the summer of 1997, word leaked to the media, and the gun supporters in Pennsylvania pounded Rendell into political pulp.

Kairys resigned from his city position earlier this year. But he has published his views in the upcoming *Temple Law Review*. News of his proposal reached mayors in Chicago, Detroit and Miami, who are considering suing the gun companies.

The cover is about to be blown off an industry that has caused immeasurable damage. It is about time.

[As of January 1999, New Orleans, Chicago, Miami and Bridgeport, Connecticut have followed Professor Kairys' prescription and sued gun manufacturers to recover the costs of medical treatment for gunshot victims and for law enforcement expenses related to gun crimes. The National Rifle Association is pushing legislation in Congress that would limit these lawsuits.]

Democracy and
Product Liability Deform

July 2, 1998

While President Clinton instructs China on the merits of democracy, back on 1600 Pennsylvania Avenue the president and his staff have cut a deal to erode one of the fundamental pillars of American democracy: the civil justice system.

The White House has signed off on legislation introduced by Senators Slade Gorton, R-Washington, and Jay Rockefeller, D-West Virginia, (a major recipient of corporate PAC money with more than $1 million from 1995 to 1996) to give business a breakthrough victory in its long-running crusade to eliminate consumers' ability to hold companies accountable through the tort system for selling dangerous products.

Business hates citizen access to the tort system for several crucial reasons.

First, it provides citizens with a direct means to hold manufacturers of dangerous products responsible for the harm they cause. Consumers injured by a dangerous medical device, for example, do not have to petition the Food and Drug Administration and wait for the federal agency to act. They can sue the company directly, and let the case be decided by a jury of their peers.

Second, the civil justice system's discovery process—which provides an injured party suing a manufacturer with the right to demand copies of internal company documents—gets corporate dirty secrets out into the open. As the documents discovered in tobacco litigation illustrate, airing those dirty secrets often spurs civic, regulatory and legislative initiatives to force changes in corporate manufacturing and other practices.

Third, jury verdicts, while generally conservative, are relatively unpredictable. And in the case of egregious corporate conduct, there is always the possibility of a large punitive damages award.

To erode public support for the civil justice system, Big Business has waged a high-priced, deceitful propaganda effort. Corporate flacks and rented experts spread misleading and sometimes fraudulent anecdotes to discredit the system. They point to an explosion in product liability litigation, though in fact product liability suits make up only approximately 0.2 percent of all civil cases filed in stated courts. They allege punitive damage awards regularly threaten companies' well being—even though there are only about 13 punitive damages awards a year in federal and state products liability suits.

The Rockefeller-Gorton-White House bill would not give business everything it wants in products liability deform, but it is a far-reaching and dangerous start. Among its key provisions:

- A $250,000 cap on punitive damages for businesses with fewer than 25 employees and less than $5 million in annual revenues. Small business may deserve some breaks from government—but not an effective exemption from one of the most important deterrents to corporate wrongdoing. This is especially the case given the hazards posed by small gun makers, fireworks manufacturers and others. In any case, if small business gets the exemption, big business will immediately demand it be extended to large companies as well.

- A sharp limit on company liability for durable goods used in the workplace and intended to last for a long time (for example, machinery, elevators). Under the bill, workers injured by the defective product could not sue the product manufacturer if the elevator, machine or other item was more than 18 years old and the worker's injury was covered—however inadequately—by workers' compensation.

- A massive cutback in liability for sellers of dangerous products. Consumers will now have the burden of showing that a seller operated negligently in selling a dangerous product (for example, by selling an item they should have known was defective). Sellers will no longer have a duty to inform customers of known product defects.

These and other provisions would preempt state law, making a mockery of Congressional Republicans' purported agenda of devolving power to the states.

However, many Big Business factions—including the Auto Manufacturers Association, the Chemical Manufacturers Association and the American Petroleum Institute—are actually opposing the bill, which they claim does not go far enough and contains some provisions that might interfere with state efforts to limit consumers' rights. An ironic Big Business-consumer group coalition may yet engineer the bill's defeat.

Senate Majority Leader Trent Lott has announced that he intends to ram the bill through Senate, by cutting off debate—before it has even begun—as the first order of business when the Senate returns after its July 4 break. If the Senate approves the bill, the House of Representatives is expected to follow in short order.

The Gorton-Rockefeller-White House bill would significantly close off citizen access to the court house, blocking perhaps the chief means of direct democracy in the United States. The Senate can offer a genuine lesson in democracy by defeating Lott's attempt to cut off debate on the bill (with a "no" vote on cloture), and then voting it down.

[The alliance between the Big Business tort deform hardliners and consumer groups and other defenders of the civil justice system prevailed in 1998, and the Rockefeller-Gorton-White House bill failed to pass.]

Dissolving Unocal

September 15, 1998

The mainstream view among citizen activists is that the most effective means of dealing with corporate crime and violence is through regulation, litigation, legislation and law enforcement.

But a breakaway group of activists want to move directly to a sanction that will get the attention of every big corporation in America—revocation of the charters of the most egregious of corporate wrongdoers.

Throughout the nation's history, the states have had the authority to give birth to a corporation by granting a corporate charter and to impose the death penalty on a corporate wrongdoer by revoking its charter.

Earlier today, a coalition of more than thirty public interest organizations called on the attorney general of California to revoke the charter of Union Oil of California (Unocal).

Why Unocal?

The 127-page petition argued that Unocal was a recidivist corporation, engaged in corporate law-breaking, was responsible for the 1969 oil blowout in the Santa Barbara Channel and numerous other acts of pollution, committed hundreds of OSHA violations, treated workers unfairly, is complicit in human rights violations in Afghanistan and Burma, and has "usurped political power."

Arguing that the state of California routinely puts out of business hundreds of unruly accountants, lawyers and doctors every year, the coalition called upon California AG Dan Lungren, who is running for governor, to revoke Unocal's charter.

"We're letting the people of California in on a well-kept secret," said Loyola Law School Professor Robert Benson, who drafted the petition. "The people mistakenly assume that we have to try to control these giant corporate repeat offenders one toxic spill at a time, one layoff at a time, one human rights violation at a time. But the law has always allowed the attorney general to go to court to simply dissolve a corporation for wrongdoing and sell its assets to others who will operate in the public interest."

If this authority exists, why is it that only once this century—in 1976 when a conservative Republican AG asked a court to dissolve a private water company for allegedly delivering impure water to its customers—has the attorney general sought to revoke a corporate charter in California?

"California attorneys general haven't often done it because they've become soft on corporate crime," Benson answers. "Baseball players and convicted individuals in California get only three strikes. Why should big corporations get endless strikes?"

Benson argues that a single act of unlawfulness is enough to trigger charter revocation proceedings, although he admits that if an attorney general acts against a major company, it will be for a pattern of wrongdoing, not for an isolated act of wrongdoing.

But Unocal's Barry Lane argues that if it is true that one bad act can trigger revocation, then "any company that has ever been found guilty of anything," would face charter revocation proceedings and "the AG would be running every company in the state."

So, which is Unocal—a sometimes criminal, or a corporate recidivist?

"We have committed misdemeanors in the past," Lane admits, "but then so have many companies. We have operated here for 100 years. Yes, we have made some mistakes, but we have always taken responsibility for those mistakes and worked to correct them."

And the company has a friend in the attorney general. Lungren is on the cover of the current issue of William Buckley's *National Review*, under the headline "Great Right Hope."

In other words, the chances are slim to none that Lungren will move against his pals in the oil industry. So, why file the petition?

"We are not politically naive," Benson answers. "We don't think that this is going to get so far along the road that Unocal will actually be broken up anytime soon, although it should be. Much more likely, we think the attorney general will deny the petition, and then we will use this as a tool to put pressure on the political process."

If an attorney general were independent enough to file such a petition, a judge could appoint a receiver, so that the assets do not flee the jurisdiction. Then if the judge has the guts to strip the company of its charter, he has the authority to make "such orders and decrees and issue such injunctions in the case as justice and equity require."

If Benson were the judge, he'd transform the company into a renewable energy company, which would create more jobs and inflict less damage to the environment.

But Benson is not the judge and he admits that Unocal will not lose its charter anytime soon. The petition was filed to spur change in our stagnant legal and political culture, so that, as Benson says, "some day in the future we will dissolve Unocal and other giant corporate repeat offenders."

[The Attorney General of California rejected the petition to revoke Unocal's charter a scant five days after it was filed— hardly enough time to review a 127-page document. Professor Benson is planning an appeal. "We got a three sentence rejection that a court can clearly reverse as arbitrary and capricious," he said.]

Smoked Out: The Attorneys General Cave In to Big Tobacco

November 23, 1998

They've done it again.

Faced with unprecedented risk in the face of innovative lawsuits from 40 U.S. states, Big Tobacco and its lawyers have again concocted a national settlement proposal that will enable the industry to escape from its current difficulties.

The deal—now accepted by 46 states, the District of Columbia and four territories—purports to offer just over $200 billion to the states over a 25-year period plus some minor public health concessions in exchange for the states dropping their claims.

Without knowing more, the proposal can immediately be identified as an industry-protection deal by the single fact that the companies gave states just a week to accept the deal, on a take-it-or-leave-it basis.

The only possible explanation for this arbitrary time limit is that the industry did not want the state attorneys general who signed the deal—and definitely not the public—to understand what is in the proposed agreement. The settlement proposal is more than 100 pages of complicated, confusing and technical legal jargon. There was no way to analyze it fully and carefully in a week.

Still, a quick review is enough to show how weak and harmful the deal is.

First, the $200 billion figure is inflated. Industry payments will be tax deductible. Since they are so spread out and higher payments come later, the real cost to the companies is less. The payments are less on a per capita basis than Minnesota received in its individual settlement. Most importantly, the $200 billion would only cover about one-third of the Medicaid costs incurred due to smoking-related disease—it was to recover these costs that the states brought their suits.

Second, the proposal's public health provisions are laughably weak and riddled with loopholes. Instead of banning industry sponsorships, it will permit each company to sponsor one sports event or concert series a year. It bans the use of most cartoons (though remember, Joe Camel is already retired in the United States), but permits the continued use of human images—meaning the Marlboro Man will continue to convey the values of ruggedness and freedom to lure children into enslavement to nicotine addiction and its attendant consequences of disease and death.

There is little question that, under the deal, Big Tobacco will continue to spend at least as much on promotion and marketing as it does now. The main consequence of the settlement agreement will be to funnel it away from billboard advertisements (most of which are banned) to other outlets.

The deal does not contain "look-back" provisions, which would make the tobacco companies responsible for reducing youth smoking rates, and penalize them if they failed.

Third, the deal contains several provisions which are out-and-out harmful. The overly broad settlement language will prevent states from filing important health-related suits against the industry in the future. States will be barred, for example, from suing the tobacco companies to recover the medical-care costs associated with second-hand smoke.

Outrageously, the deal will also block local governments from filing a wide array of suits against the industry, and may even impede city and county governments' ability to enforce local tobacco-related ordinances.

The worst part of the deal may be a provision that will cut the mandated industry payments if the federal government taxes the tobacco companies and then gives some of the resulting revenue to the states. There is no way the federal government is going to give money to the states if those payments will only serve to reduce industry's payments to the states. And politically it will be very difficult for Congress to pass a cigarette tax increase if it cannot transfer some of the revenue to the states.

Thus, in cutting a deal with the states, Big Tobacco may succeed in blocking federal action to address the smoking problem.

Despite all these problems, however, the current settlement is still a step up from the deal proposed last year. Crucially, this settlement does not interfere with the ability of individuals to sue the tobacco companies, either on their own or in class actions.

The tragedy of the current tobacco deal is that there was an alternative approach available. Each state could have continued preparing its case, and brought it to trial or settled it individually.

The four states that settled before the multistate agreement each included a "most favored nation" provision in their settlements. Those provisions stipulated that any better terms provided to later settling states would automatically be given to the earlier settling states.

This created a situation where each state was able to build on the settlement that came before, getting a bit more money or adding a new public health provision. This more cautious approach meant that mistakes in one settlement could be fixed in the next, and the industry did not have the chance to bamboozle the states, as it has now done. And, the state-by-state approach denied Big Tobacco a once-and-for all settlement that helps afford the tobacco companies the litigation peace they so desperately crave.

Index

About the Authors

Russell Mokhiber is editor of *Corporate Crime Reporter*, a legal weekly based in Washington, DC. He is also author of *Corporate Crime and Violence*.

Robert Weissman is editor of the Washington DC-based *Multinational Monitor*, the leading source of critical reporting on corporate power. He is also co-director of Essential Action, a corporate accountability group.

For More Great Info

Corporate Predators is a compendium of the "Focus on the Corporation" column written by Russell Mokhiber and Robert Weissman. If you would like to receive a free electronic subscription to the weekly column, send an e-mail message to listproc@essential.org. In the text of the message, include the following all in one line:

subscribe corp-focus <your name> (no period).

Subscriptions to *Multinational Monitor* magazine are available for $25/year from:

Multinational Monitor
P.O. Box 19405
Washington, D.C. 20036
Tel: 202-387-8030
Fax: 202-234-5176
E-mail: monitor@essential.org

Or, visit the *Multinational Monitor* web site at <www.essential.org/monitor>.